SAXON MATH™

Intermediate 5

Assessment Guide

Stephen Hake

A Harcourt Achieve Imprint

www.SaxonPublishers.com

1-800-284-7019

Printed in the U.S.A.

ISBN 978-1-600-32364-5

8 9 10 0982 20 19 18 17 16 15 14

4500464428 ^ B C D E F G

Assessment Guide

***Saxon Math** Intermediate 5 Assessment Guide* contains Course Assessments, Cumulative Test Answer Forms, and Test Analysis Forms. Descriptions of these components are provided below.

About the Placement Test

The Placement Test is a forty-problem test that can be used to help you find the best initial placement for students who are new to the ***Saxon Math*** program. The test contains selected content from *Intermediate 3, Intermediate 4, Intermediate 5, and Course 1.* Placement Test instructions are provided on page 5 of this booklet. A scoring guide is provided on page 9. **The Placement Test is not intended for use with current *Saxon Math* students.**

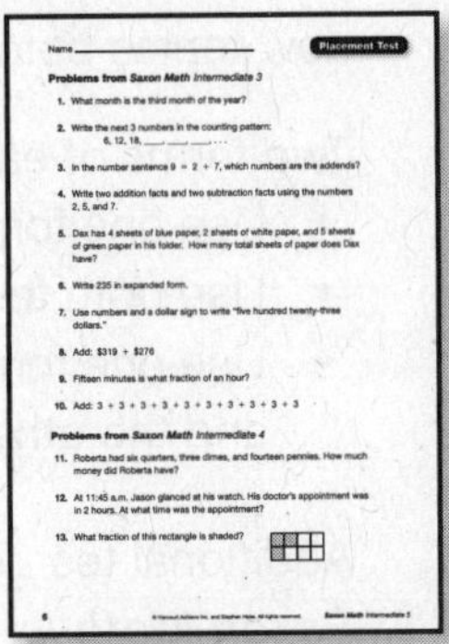

Placement Test

About the Baseline Test

A multiple-choice Baseline Test for ***Saxon Math** Intermediate 5* is included. Administer this fifty-problem test once early in the school year to gauge the skills of incoming students. The content covers skills and concepts that are included in the math curriculum of the preceding year.

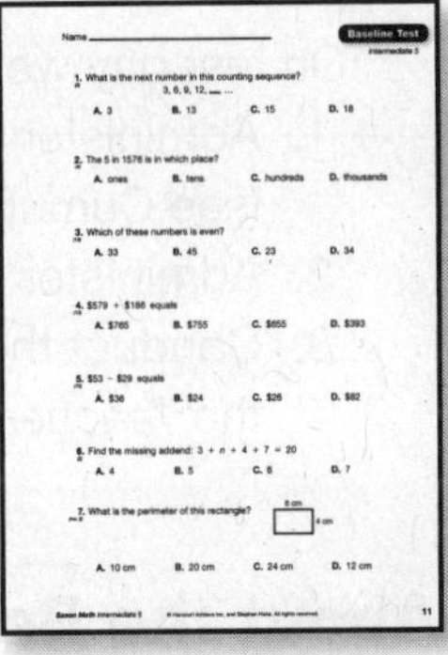

Baseline Test

About the Power-Up Tests

Power-Up Tests are administered with the Cumulative Tests. Each Cumulative Test identifies the Power-Up Test to be taken that day. Every Power-Up Test contains a Facts section and a Problem-Solving section. The Power-Up Tests are designed to assess students' ability to quickly recall basic facts, demonstrate basic skills, implement problem-solving strategies, and communicate mathematical ideas. We suggest timing students on the Facts portion of the Power-Up Test, allowing a maximum of three minutes. Students may complete the Problem-Solving portion of the Power-Up Test at their own pace.

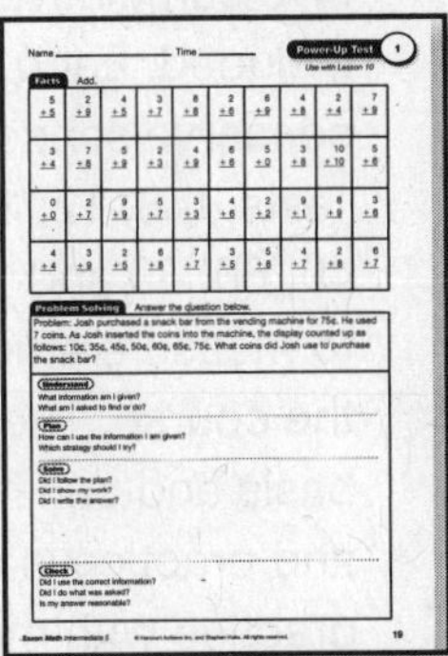

Power-Up Test

About the Cumulative Tests

The Cumulative Tests are designed to reward students and to provide teachers with diagnostic information. The Cumulative Test design allows students to demonstrate the skills they have developed, and it fosters confidence that will benefit students when they encounter comprehensive standardized tests.

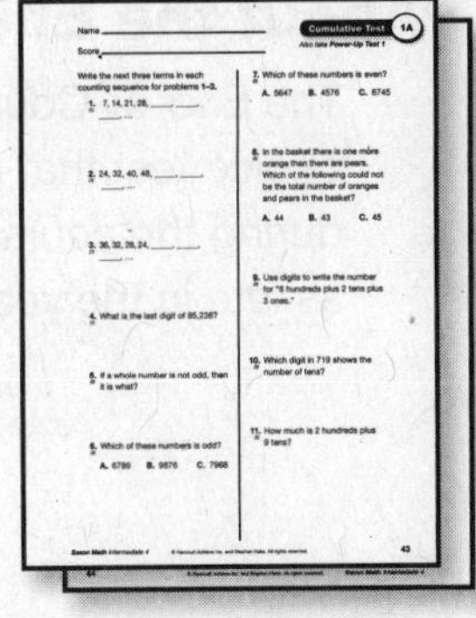

Cumulative Test

Schedule

Cumulative Tests should be given after every fifth lesson, beginning after Lesson 10. The testing schedule is explained in greater detail on page 4 of this book.

Administering the Cumulative Tests according to the schedule is essential. Following the schedule allows students sufficient practice on new topics before they are assessed on those topics.

Two forms of each test are included, providing the following options:

- Use one form as an original test and the other as a makeup test.
- Use both forms on test day to discourage copying.
- Use one form as an in-class practice (cooperative work acceptable) and the other as the test.

Additional test forms may be created using the ***Saxon Math*** *Intermediate 5 Test and Practice Generator.*

Test Day

On test day we recommend three activities:

1. Administer the Power-Up Test indicated in the *Teacher's Manual* (see Cumulative Assessment page) or on the Cumulative Test.
2. Administer the Cumulative Test.
3. Conduct the Performance Task or Test-day Activity suggested in the *Teacher's Manual* (see Performance Assessment page).

About the Benchmark Tests

Five cumulative Benchmark Tests for ***Saxon Math*** *Intermediate 5* are included. Each contains twenty-five multiple-choice problems. To conserve school days, these tests may be used in lieu of Cumulative Tests 4, 8, 12, 16, and 20, which cover content through Lessons 20, 40, 60, 80 and 100 respectively. The Benchmark Tests are designed to measure student comprehension of topics previously introduced in the course. They provide a measure of student progress on a regular basis and can help identify concepts for which additional instruction and practice is indicated. The Benchmark Tests also provide additional practice with multiple-choice items. Familiarity with this format will lead to success on standardized assessment tests.

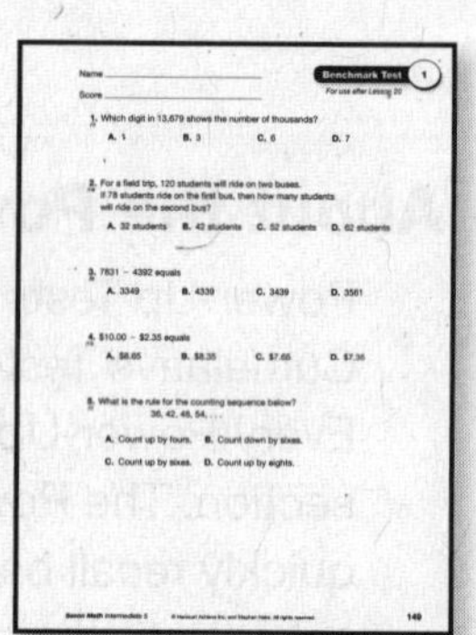
Benchmark Test

About the End-of-Course Exam

The End-of-Course Exam is a comprehensive, fifty-problem, multiple-choice test that assesses student knowledge of the content presented during the course. This cumulative assessment should be administered as late in the year as possible.

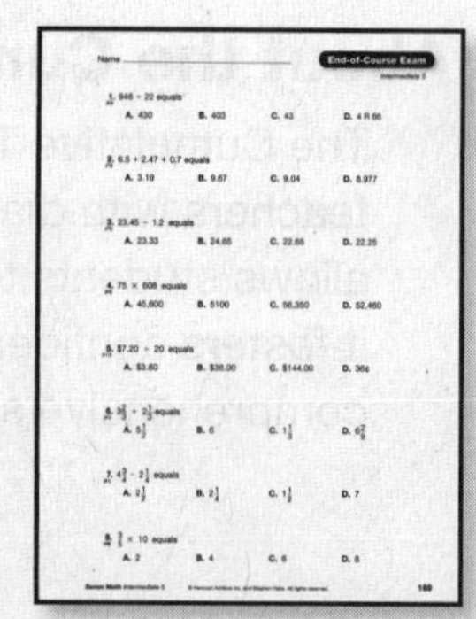
End-of-Course Exam

About the Test Solution Answer Forms

This book contains three kinds of answer forms for the Cumulative Tests that you might find useful. These answer forms provide sufficient space for students to record their work on Cumulative Tests.

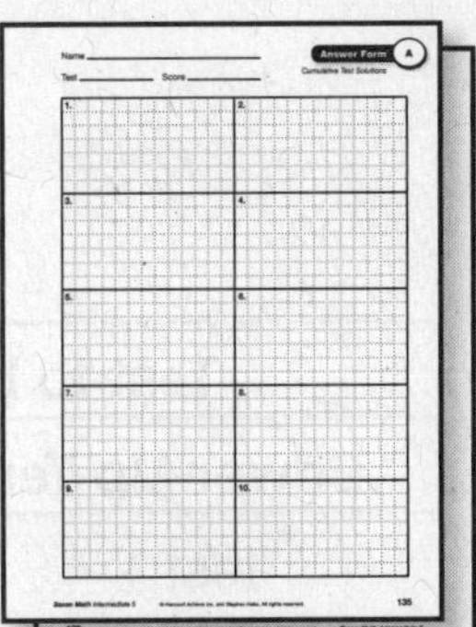

Answer Form A

Answer Form A: Cumulative Test Solutions

This is a double-sided master with a grid background and partitions for recording the solutions to twenty problems.

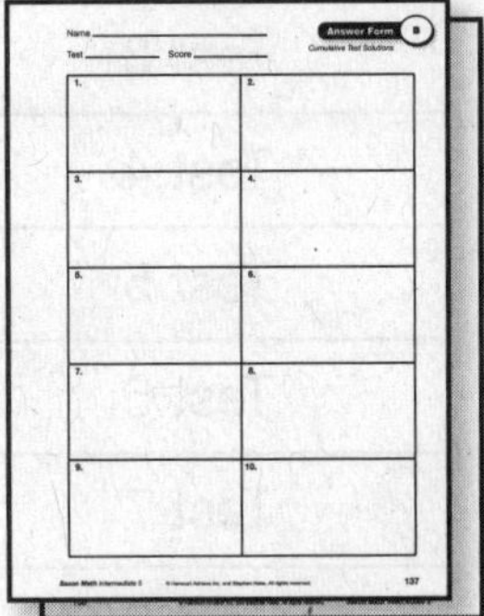

Answer Form B

Answer Form B: Cumulative Test Solutions

This is a double-sided master with a plain, white background and partitions for recording the solutions to twenty problems.

Answer Form C: Cumulative Test Solutions

This is a single-sided master with partitions for recording the solutions to twenty problems and a separate answer column on the right-hand side.

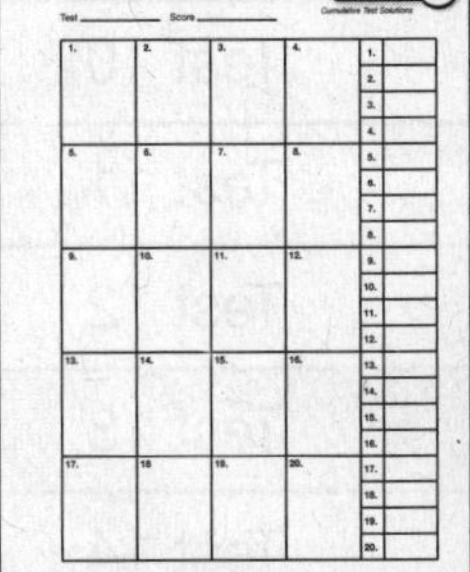

Answer Form C

About the Test Analysis Forms

The Cumulative Test Analysis Forms are designed to help you track and analyze student performance on the Cumulative Tests.

Class Test Analysis Form A

Beginning with Cumulative Test 1, record those test items that students have missed. By reviewing the column for items that appear repeatedly, you can quickly determine which test items are causing students the most trouble. Update this form after every test to determine for which concepts additional instruction or practice may be necessary.

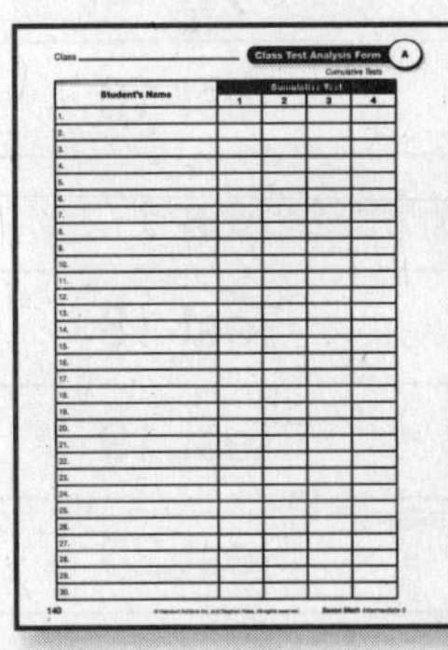

Class Test Analysis Form A

Individual Test Analysis Form B

This form cross-references every Cumulative Test item with the lesson where the concept was introduced. Complete a separate form after every test for each student who scored below 80%. Circle the corresponding lesson for every item missed. Not all students will have mastered a new concept at the time it is first assessed. However, if a student has not mastered a concept after repeated practice and assessment, then reteaching is indicated. This form allows you to identify the student's misunderstandings and plan remediation activities.

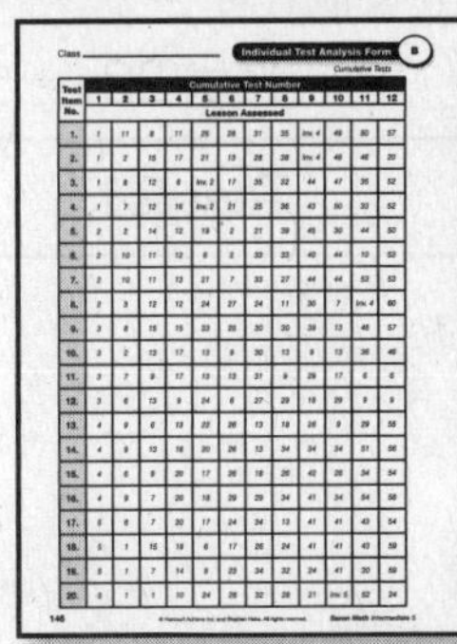

Individual Test Analysis Form B

Testing Schedule

Test to be administered:		Covers material through	Give after teaching
Power-Up Test	Cumulative Test		
Test 1	Test 1	Lesson 5	Lesson 10
Test 2	Test 2	Lesson 10	Lesson 15
Test 3	Test 3	Lesson 15	Lesson 20
Test 4	Test 4	Lesson 20	Lesson 25
Test 5	Test 5	Lesson 25	Lesson 30
Test 6	Test 6	Lesson 30	Lesson 35
Test 7	Test 7	Lesson 35	Lesson 40
Test 8	Test 8	Lesson 40	Lesson 45
Test 9	Test 9	Lesson 45	Lesson 50
Test 10	Test 10	Lesson 50	Lesson 55
Test 11	Test 11	Lesson 55	Lesson 60
Test 12	Test 12	Lesson 60	Lesson 65
Test 13	Test 13	Lesson 65	Lesson 70
Test 14	Test 14	Lesson 70	Lesson 75
Test 15	Test 15	Lesson 75	Lesson 80
Test 16	Test 16	Lesson 80	Lesson 85
Test 17	Test 17	Lesson 85	Lesson 90
Test 18	Test 18	Lesson 90	Lesson 95
Test 19	Test 19	Lesson 95	Lesson 100
Test 20	Test 20	Lesson 100	Lesson 105
Test 21	Test 21	Lesson 105	Lesson 110
Test 22	Test 22	Lesson 110	Lesson 115
Test 23	Test 23	Lesson 115	Lesson 120

*Use this test to help determine correct placement within the **Saxon Math** Intermediate and/or Courses 1, 2, and 3 textbook series.*

The Placement Test may be of assistance in placing some students. Please note that this test is simply a tool to assist teachers in the initial placement of their students. **This test should not be used to determine whether a student already using the Saxon program should skip a textbook.** Allow the student one hour to take the test (or until he or she cannot work any more problems). The student should work without assistance and show all work. Calculators may not be used during the test.

Look over the student's work carefully, grade the test, and use the guidelines below to place the student. An online version of the Placement Test is available at **www.SaxonPublishers.com.**

Placement Test Guidelines

4 or fewer correct from problems 1–10 and student is an average-to-accelerated third-grader	Student may begin ***Saxon Math** Intermediate 3.*
5 or more correct from problems 1–10	Student may begin ***Saxon Math** Intermediate 4.*
7 or more correct from problems 1–10 and **5 or more correct** from problems 11–20	Student may begin ***Saxon Math** Intermediate 5.*
7 or more correct from problems 11–20 and **5 or more correct** from problems 21–30 and **any correct** from problems 31–40	Student may begin ***Saxon Math** Course 1.*

Name ____________________

Placement Test

Problems from *Saxon Math* Intermediate 3

1. What month is the third month of the year?

2. Write the next 3 numbers in the counting pattern:
   6, 12, 18, ____, ____, ____, . . .

3. In the number sentence $9 = 2 + 7$, which numbers are the addends?

4. Write two addition facts and two subtraction facts using the numbers 2, 5, and 7.

5. Dax has 4 sheets of blue paper, 2 sheets of white paper, and 5 sheets of green paper in his folder. How many total sheets of paper does Dax have?

6. Write 235 in expanded form.

7. Use numbers and a dollar sign to write "five hundred twenty-three dollars."

8. Add: $319 + $276

9. Fifteen minutes is what fraction of an hour?

10. Add: $3 + 3 + 3 + 3 + 3 + 3 + 3 + 3 + 3 + 3$

Problems from *Saxon Math* Intermediate 4

11. Roberta had six quarters, three dimes, and fourteen pennies. How much money did Roberta have?

12. At 11:45 a.m. Jason glanced at his watch. His doctor's appointment was in 2 hours. At what time was the appointment?

13. What fraction of this rectangle is shaded?

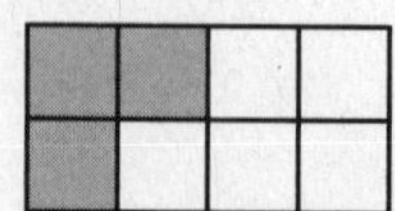

14. What is the perimeter of this rectangle?

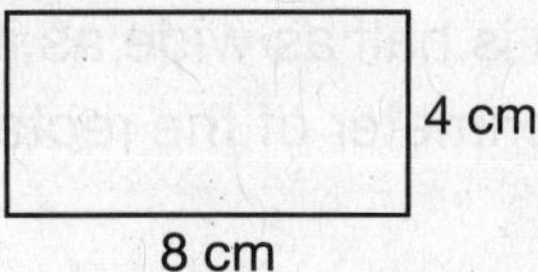

15. Three feet equals one yard. A car that is 15 feet long is how many yards long?

16. 346×90

17. $\$20.00 - \$17.84$

18. $4\overline{)1480}$

19. 48 + 163 + 9 + 83

20. How long is this line segment?

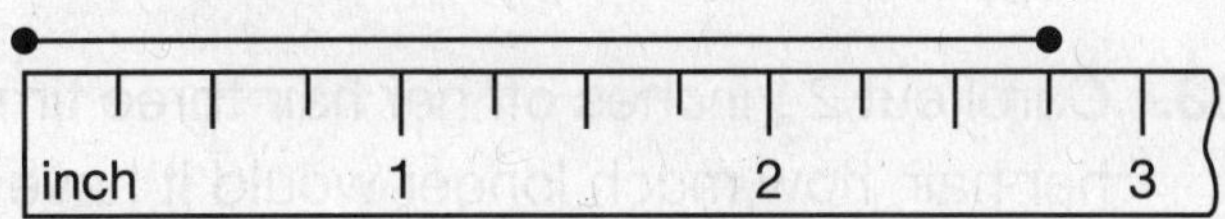

Problems from *Saxon Math* Intermediate 5

21. Carlos gave the clerk a $10 bill for a book that cost $6.95 plus $0.42 tax. How much money should Carlos get back from the clerk?

22. The distance around the school track is $\frac{1}{4}$ mile. How many times around the track does Cheryl need to run in order to run one mile?

23. Estimate the product of 67 and 73 by rounding each number to the nearest ten before multiplying.

24. In 2 hours the 3 boys picked a total of 1347 cherries. If they share the cherries equally, then how many cherries will each boy keep?

25. 67×89

26. $4608 - 2729$

27. $60\overline{)1590}$

28. 2.25 + 12.7

29. $5\frac{3}{4} + 2\frac{3}{4}$

30. This rectangle is half as wide as it is long. What is the perimeter of the rectangle?

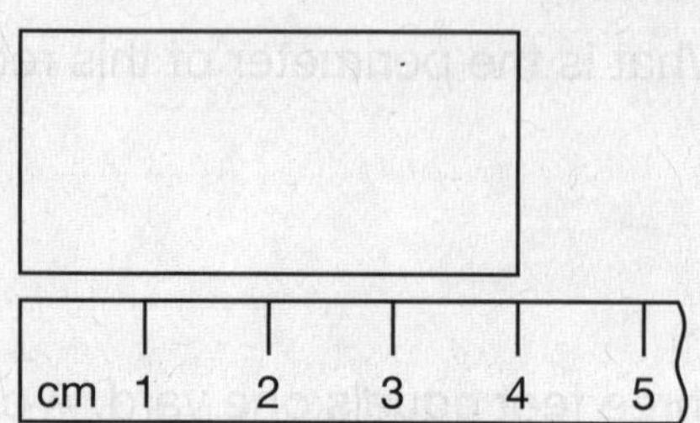

Problems from *Saxon Math* Course 1

31. New York City uses about one billion, three hundred million gallons of water each day. Use digits to write that number.

32. Jill is on page 42 of a 180-page book. If she must finish the book in three days, then she needs to read an average of how many pages each day?

33. Carol cut $2\frac{1}{2}$ inches off her hair three times last year. If she had not cut her hair, how much longer would it have been at the end of the year?

34. One half of the area of the square is shaded. What is the area of the shaded region?

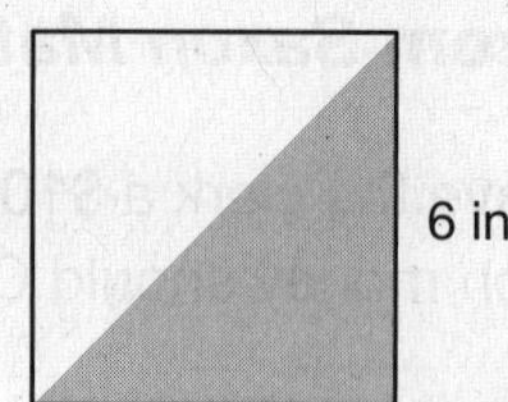

35. $2\frac{1}{3} + 1\frac{3}{4}$

36. 6.3×0.48

37. $6.7 + 0.48$

38. $\frac{5}{8} \times \frac{3}{5}$

39. $6.3 \div 9$

40. If $n - 72 = 36$, what is the value of n?

Name ____________________ Recommended placement ____________________

Grade ____________________ School ____________________

Date tested ____________________

Directions: For each correct answer, place a check mark in the corresponding box. For each section, count the number of correct answers. Place the student according to the placement information for that section.

Scorecard	Number of Correct Answers	Placement Test Guidelines
1. ☐ 2. ☐ 3. ☐ 4. ☐ 5. ☐ 6. ☐ 7. ☐ 8. ☐ 9. ☐ 10. ☐	______	**Four or fewer correct from 1–10:** 1. Average-to-accelerated fourth-grader: Begin *Intermediate 4.* 2. Below average fourth-grader: Consider *Intermediate 3.* **Five or more correct from 1–10:** Begin *Intermediate 4.*
11. ☐ 12. ☐ 13. ☐ 14. ☐ 15. ☐ 16. ☐ 17. ☐ 18. ☐ 19. ☐ 20. ☐	______	**Seven or more correct from 1–10 and five or more correct from 11–20:** Begin *Intermediate 5.*
21. ☐ 22. ☐ 23. ☐ 24. ☐ 25. ☐ 26. ☐ 27. ☐ 28. ☐ 29. ☐ 30. ☐	______	**Seven or more correct from 11–20 and five or more correct from 21–30:** Accelerated fourth-grader or average fifth-grader: Begin *Intermediate 5.*
31. ☐ 32. ☐ 33. ☐ 34. ☐ 35. ☐ 36. ☐ 37. ☐ 38. ☐ 39. ☐ 40. ☐	______	**Seven or more correct from 11–20 and five or more correct from 21–30 and any correct from 31–40:** Begin *Course 1.*

1. March
2. 24, 30, 36
3. 2 and 7
4. $2 + 5 = 7$, $5 + 2 = 7$,
   $7 - 2 = 5$, $7 - 5 = 2$
5. 11
6. $200 + 30 + 5$
7. $523
8. $595
9. $\frac{1}{4}$
10. 30
11. $1.94
12. 1:45 p.m.
13. $\frac{3}{8}$
14. 24 cm
15. 5 yards
16. 31,140
17. $2.16
18. 370
19. 303
20. $2\frac{3}{4}$ inches
21. $2.63
22. 4 times
23. 4900
24. 449 cherries
25. 5963
26. 1879
27. 26 R 30 or $26\frac{1}{2}$ or 26.5
28. 14.95
29. $8\frac{1}{2}$
30. 12 cm
31. 1,300,000,000
32. 46 pages
33. $7\frac{1}{2}$ in.
34. 18 sq. in. or 18 $in.^2$
35. $4\frac{1}{12}$
36. 3.024
37. 7.18
38. $\frac{3}{8}$
39. 0.7
40. 108

Name ____________________

Baseline Test

Intermediate 5

1. What is the next number in this counting sequence?
(3)

3, 6, 9, 12, ___, ...

A. 3 **B.** 13 **C.** 15 **D.** 18

2. The 5 in 1576 is in which place?
(4)

A. ones **B.** tens **C.** hundreds **D.** thousands

3. Which of these numbers is even?
(10)

A. 33 **B.** 45 **C.** 23 **D.** 34

4. \$579 + \$186 equals
(13)

A. \$765 **B.** \$755 **C.** \$655 **D.** \$393

5. \$53 − \$29 equals
(15)

A. \$36 **B.** \$24 **C.** \$26 **D.** \$82

6. Find the missing addend: $3 + n + 4 + 7 = 20$
(2)

A. 4 **B.** 5 **C.** 6 **D.** 7

7. What is the perimeter of this rectangle?
(Inv. 2)

6 cm
4 cm

A. 10 cm **B.** 20 cm **C.** 24 cm **D.** 12 cm

8. Which arrow could be pointing to 83 on this number line?
(Inv. 1)

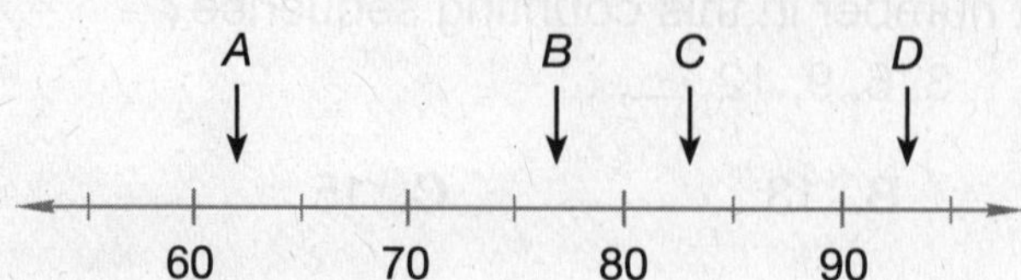

A. arrow *A** **B.** arrow *B* **C.** arrow *C* **D.** arrow *D*

9. Which of these angles appears to be a right angle?
(23)

A. 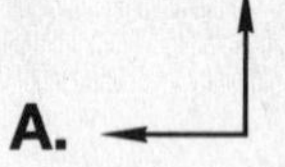 **B.**  **C.** **D.**

10. What fraction of this rectangle is shaded? 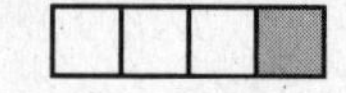
(22)

A. $\frac{1}{3}$ **B.** $\frac{1}{4}$ **C.** $\frac{3}{4}$ **D.** $\frac{1}{5}$

11. What is the area of this rectangle?
(Inv. 3)

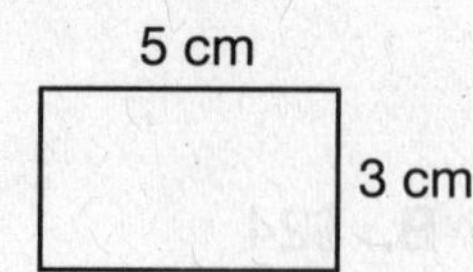

A. 16 sq. cm **B.** 15 sq. cm **C.** 8 sq. cm **D.** 30 sq. cm

12. How do you express *twelve million, five hundred forty thousand* using digits?
(34)

A. 12,540,000 **B.** 12,500,040 **C.** 125,004,000 **D.** 12,000,540

13. 8 × 7 equals
(38)

A. 15 **B.** 55 **C.** 56 **D.** 64

14. How long is this segment?
(39)

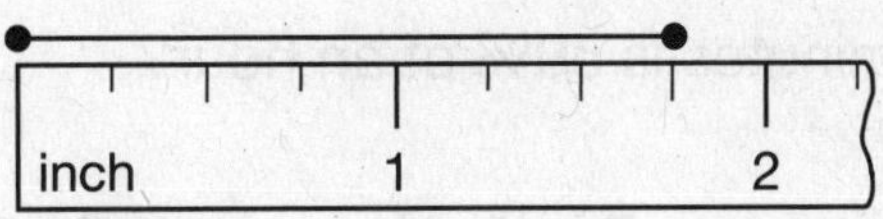

A. $1\frac{3}{8}$ in. **B.** $\frac{7}{8}$ in. **C.** $2\frac{1}{4}$ in. **D.** $1\frac{3}{4}$ in.

15. How many quarts equal one gallon?
(40)

A. 2 quarts **B.** 4 quarts **C.** 8 quarts **D.** $\frac{1}{4}$ quart

16. \$5.00 − \$1.38 equals
(41)

A. \$3.62 **B.** \$3.72 **C.** \$4.38 **D.** \$6.38

17. 9 − (6 − 3) equals
(45)

A. 0 **B.** 3 **C.** 6 **D.** 9

18. \$25 × 7 equals
(48)

A. \$1.75 **B.** \$175 **C.** \$145 **D.** \$32

19. Four dozen eggs is how many eggs?
(49)

A. 4 eggs **B.** 16 eggs **C.** 40 eggs **D.** 48 eggs

20. 3.75 + 12.4 equals
(50)

A. 16.15 **B.** 4.99 **C.** 15.79 **D.** 15.15

21. How many minutes is 50% of an hour?
(Inv. 5)

A. 50 minutes **B.** 40 minutes **C.** 30 minutes **D.** 20 minutes

22. If 5280 is rounded to the nearest hundred, the result is ________.
(42)

A. 6000 **B.** 5000 **C.** 5200 **D.** 5300

23. Which of these numbers is not a factor of 12?
(55)

A. 2 **B.** 3 **C.** 4 **D.** 5

24. Which comparison is correct?
(56)

A. $\frac{1}{2} > \frac{1}{4}$ **B.** $\frac{1}{2} < \frac{1}{4}$ **C.** $\frac{1}{4} > \frac{1}{2}$ **D.** $\frac{1}{2} = \frac{1}{4}$

25. Donna drove 60 miles in one hour. At that rate, how far could Donna drive in 3 hours?
(57)

A. 20 mi **B.** 63 mi **C.** 120 mi **D.** 180 mi

26. Estimate the product of 38 and 53 by rounding each number to the nearest ten before multiplying.
(59)

A. 1500 **B.** 2000 **C.** 1800 **D.** 2400

27. If $\frac{3}{5}$ of the students in the class are boys, then what fraction of the students are girls?
(61)

A. $\frac{2}{5}$ **B.** $\frac{3}{5}$ **C.** $\frac{5}{3}$ **D.** $\frac{3}{8}$

28. 8^2 equals
(62)

A. 4 **B.** 16 **C.** 64 **D.** 82

29. Which word names this polygon?
(63)

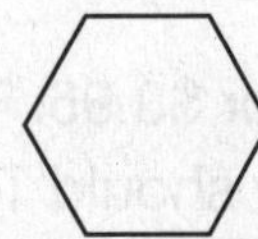

A. decagon **B.** hexagon **C.** octagon **D.** quadrilateral

30. 72 ÷ 3 equals
(64)

A. 20 R 2 **B.** 114 **C.** 42 **D.** 24

31. The line segment is 2 cm long. How many millimeters long is it?
(69)

A. 2 mm **B.** 20 mm **C.** 0.2 mm **D.** 200 mm

32. Which weight best describes your math book?
(77)

A. 1 kilogram **B.** 1 gram **C.** 1 ounce **D.** 1 ton

33. Which of these triangles appears to be equilateral?
(78)

A. 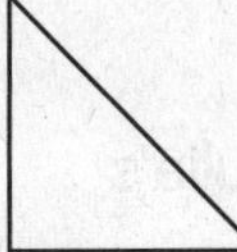 **B.**  **C.** 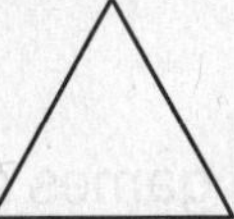 **D.** 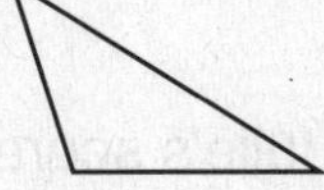

34. 615 ÷ 3 equals
(80)

A. 25 **B.** 205 **C.** 215 **D.** 2005

35. Which of these angles appears to be a 90° angle?
(81)

A. **B.** **C.** **D.**

36. Todd bought a model car for $3.95. The sales tax was 32¢. He paid with a $5 bill. How much money should Todd get back?
(83)

A. $4.27 **B.** $0.73 **C.** $1.73 **D.** $1.37

37. $36.00 × 10 equals
(85)

A. $3.60 **B.** $36.00 **C.** $360.00 **D.** $3600.00

38. 36 × 27 equals
(90)

A. 7452 **B.** 1272 **C.** 1132 **D.** 972

39. Which word names this polygon?
(63, 92)

A. hexagon **B.** rectangle **C.** parallelogram **D.** pentagon

40. Two fifths of the 20 students earned an A on the test. How many students earned an A?
(95)

A. 6 students **B.** 8 students **C.** 10 students **D.** 12 students

41. Julie's scores on three games are 85, 85, and 100. What is Julie's average score on the three games?
(96)

A. 85 **B.** 90 **C.** 95 **D.** 100

42. McGill's game scores are 80, 85, 80, 90, and 95. What is the median of McGill's game scores?
(97)

A. 95 **B.** 90 **C.** 85 **D.** 80

43. Which word names this geometric solid?
(98)

A. cylinder **B.** cone **C.** sphere **D.** circle

44. If one regular number cube is rolled, what is the probability of rolling a 5?
(Inv. 10)

A. $\frac{1}{5}$ **B.** $\frac{1}{6}$ **C.** $\frac{5}{6}$ **D.** $\frac{1}{2}$

45. $450 \div 10$ equals
(105)

A. 45 **B.** 450 **C.** 4500 **D.** 4.5

46. Which of these fractions does not equal $\frac{1}{2}$?
(103)

A. $\frac{2}{4}$ **B.** $\frac{3}{6}$ **C.** $\frac{5}{10}$ **D.** $\frac{4}{9}$

47. $\frac{3}{7} + \frac{2}{7}$ equals
(107)

A. $\frac{5}{14}$ **B.** $\frac{1}{7}$ **C.** $\frac{5}{7}$ **D.** $\frac{5}{49}$

48. $\frac{6}{8}$ reduces to
(112)

A. $\frac{3}{4}$ **B.** $\frac{1}{2}$ **C.** $\frac{3}{8}$ **D.** $\frac{2}{3}$

49. The Roman numeral XCII equals
(Appendix B)

A. 112 **B.** 92 **C.** 1002 **D.** 42

50. Which of these numbers does not equal the fraction $\frac{3}{3}$?
(103)

A. $\frac{2}{2}$ **B.** 1 **C.** $\frac{3}{4}$ **D.** $\frac{10}{10}$

Name ________________ Time ________

Power-Up Test 1

Use with Lesson 10

Facts Add.

5 + 5	2 + 9	4 + 5	3 + 7	8 + 8	2 + 6	6 + 9	4 + 8	2 + 4	7 + 9
3 + 4	7 + 8	5 + 9	2 + 3	4 + 9	6 + 6	5 + 0	3 + 8	10 + 10	5 + 6
0 + 0	2 + 7	9 + 9	5 + 7	3 + 3	4 + 6	2 + 2	9 + 1	8 + 9	3 + 6
4 + 4	3 + 9	2 + 5	6 + 8	7 + 7	3 + 5	5 + 8	4 + 7	2 + 8	6 + 7

Problem Solving Answer the question below.

Problem: Josh purchased a snack bar from the vending machine for 75¢. He used 7 coins. As Josh inserted the coins into the machine, the display counted up as follows: 10¢, 35¢, 45¢, 50¢, 60¢, 65¢, 75¢. What coins did Josh use to purchase the snack bar?

Understand

What information am I given?
What am I asked to find or do?

Plan

How can I use the information I am given?
Which strategy should I try?

Solve

Did I follow the plan?
Did I show my work?
Did I write the answer?

Check

Did I use the correct information?
Did I do what was asked?
Is my answer reasonable?

Name ______________________ Time __________

Power-Up Test 2

Use with Lesson 15

Facts Add.

5 + 5	2 + 9	4 + 5	3 + 7	8 + 8	2 + 6	6 + 9	4 + 8	2 + 4	7 + 9
3 + 4	7 + 8	5 + 9	2 + 3	4 + 9	6 + 6	5 + 0	3 + 8	10 + 10	5 + 6
0 + 0	2 + 7	9 + 9	5 + 7	3 + 3	4 + 6	2 + 2	9 + 1	8 + 9	3 + 6
4 + 4	3 + 9	2 + 5	6 + 8	7 + 7	3 + 5	5 + 8	4 + 7	2 + 8	6 + 7

Problem Solving Answer the question below.

Problem: Matt, Clint, and Brian take turns playing pitcher for the baseball team. Matt pitched in the first game, Clint pitched in the second game, and Brian pitched in the third game. For the fourth game, Matt pitched again. If the players continue taking turns as pitcher, who will pitch in the ninth game?

Understand
What information am I given?
What am I asked to find or do?

Plan
How can I use the information I am given?
Which strategy should I try?

Solve
Did I follow the plan?
Did I show my work?
Did I write the answer?

Check
Did I use the correct information?
Did I do what was asked?
Is my answer reasonable?

Name ______________________ Time ____________

Power-Up Test 3

Use with Lesson 20

Facts

Subtract.

9 − 8	8 − 5	16 − 9	11 − 9	9 − 3	12 − 4	14 − 9	6 − 4	16 − 8	5 − 2
14 − 7	20 − 10	10 − 7	15 − 6	13 − 7	18 − 9	10 − 8	7 − 3	11 − 5	9 − 4
12 − 6	10 − 5	17 − 9	13 − 8	12 − 3	7 − 2	14 − 8	8 − 6	15 − 7	13 − 9
8 − 4	12 − 5	9 − 2	16 − 7	11 − 8	6 − 3	10 − 6	17 − 8	10 − 10	11 − 4

Problem Solving

Answer the question below.

Problem: Coins are often put into paper or plastic rolls to make their values easier to calculate. Nickels are put into rolls of 40 nickels. Pennies are put into rolls of 50 pennies. What is the value of two rolls of nickels? Two rolls of nickels have the same value as how many rolls of pennies?

Understand

What information am I given?
What am I asked to find or do?

Plan

How can I use the information I am given?
Which strategy should I try?

Solve

Did I follow the plan?
Did I show my work?
Did I write the answer?

Check

Did I use the correct information?
Did I do what was asked?
Is my answer reasonable?

Name ______________________ Time __________

Power-Up Test 4

Use with Lesson 25

Facts

Multiply.

9×6	7×1	9×2	10×10	7×4	6×5	3×2	4×4	8×6	6×3
7×7	4×3	8×5	2×2	9×9	8×3	3×0	9×7	7×2	8×8
5×4	6×2	6×6	7×3	5×5	8×7	3×3	9×8	4×2	0×7
9×4	9×5	8×2	6×4	9×3	5×2	8×4	7×5	5×3	7×6

Problem Solving

Answer the question below.

Problem: Mae-Lin has three drawers for storing clothes: a top drawer, a middle drawer, and a bottom drawer. Mae-Lin wants to put her socks in one drawer, her T-shirts in another drawer, and her jeans in another drawer. How many ways can Mae-Lin store her clothes if she puts her socks in the bottom drawer? Use diagrams to show all the ways.

Understand

What information am I given?
What am I asked to find or do?

Plan

How can I use the information I am given?
Which strategy should I try?

Solve

Did I follow the plan?
Did I show my work?
Did I write the answer?

Check

Did I use the correct information?
Did I do what was asked?
Is my answer reasonable?

Name ____________________ Time __________

Power-Up Test 5

Use with Lesson 30

Facts Add.

5 + 5	2 + 9	4 + 5	3 + 7	8 + 8	2 + 6	6 + 9	4 + 8	2 + 4	7 + 9
3 + 4	7 + 8	5 + 9	2 + 3	4 + 9	6 + 6	5 + 0	3 + 8	10 + 10	5 + 6
0 + 0	2 + 7	9 + 9	5 + 7	3 + 3	4 + 6	2 + 2	9 + 1	8 + 9	3 + 6
4 + 4	3 + 9	2 + 5	6 + 8	7 + 7	3 + 5	5 + 8	4 + 7	2 + 8	6 + 7

Problem Solving Answer the question below.

Problem: Tonight Sharise will use her telescope to observe Mars, Jupiter, and Saturn, though not necessarily in that order. What are the possible orders she can look at the three planets? (Use the abbreviations M for Mars, J for Jupiter, and S for Saturn to list the possible orders.)

Understand
What information am I given?
What am I asked to find or do?

Plan
How can I use the information I am given?
Which strategy should I try?

Solve
Did I follow the plan?
Did I show my work?
Did I write the answer?

Check
Did I use the correct information?
Did I do what was asked?
Is my answer reasonable?

Name ______________ Time ______________

Power-Up Test 6

Use with Lesson 35

Facts Subtract.

9 − 8	8 − 5	16 − 9	11 − 9	9 − 3	12 − 4	14 − 9	6 − 4	16 − 8	5 − 2
14 − 7	20 − 10	10 − 7	15 − 6	13 − 7	18 − 9	10 − 8	7 − 3	11 − 5	9 − 4
12 − 6	10 − 5	17 − 9	13 − 8	12 − 3	7 − 2	14 − 8	8 − 6	15 − 7	13 − 9
8 − 4	12 − 5	9 − 2	16 − 7	11 − 8	6 − 3	10 − 6	17 − 8	10 − 10	11 − 4

Problem Solving Answer the question below.

Problem: Half of the students on the playground were playing soccer. Half of the soccer players were girls. Half of the girls playing soccer wore red shirts. If there were 3 soccer-playing girls who wore red shirts, how many students were on the playground altogether?

Understand

What information am I given?
What am I asked to find or do?

Plan

How can I use the information I am given?
Which strategy should I try?

Solve

Did I follow the plan?
Did I show my work?
Did I write the answer?

Check

Did I use the correct information?
Did I do what was asked?
Is my answer reasonable?

Name ______________________ Time ______________

Power-Up Test 7

Use with Lesson 40

Facts Subtract.

9 − 8	8 − 5	16 − 9	11 − 9	9 − 3	12 − 4	14 − 9	6 − 4	16 − 8	5 − 2
14 − 7	20 − 10	10 − 7	15 − 6	13 − 7	18 − 9	10 − 8	7 − 3	11 − 5	9 − 4
12 − 6	10 − 5	17 − 9	13 − 8	12 − 3	7 − 2	14 − 8	8 − 6	15 − 7	13 − 9
8 − 4	12 − 5	9 − 2	16 − 7	11 − 8	6 − 3	10 − 6	17 − 8	10 − 10	11 − 4

Problem Solving Answer the question below.

Problem: Darrin, Jennifer, and Jack lined up to get on the bus. Jennifer stood right behind Jack. Darrin was not at the front of the line. In what order did the children line up?

Understand
What information am I given?
What am I asked to find or do?

Plan
How can I use the information I am given?
Which strategy should I try?

Solve
Did I follow the plan?
Did I show my work?
Did I write the answer?

Check
Did I use the correct information?
Did I do what was asked?
Is my answer reasonable?

Name ______________ Time ________

Power-Up Test 8

Use with Lesson 45

Facts Multiply.

9×6	7×1	9×2	10×10	7×4	6×5	3×2	4×4	8×6	6×3
7×7	4×3	8×5	2×2	9×9	8×3	3×0	9×7	7×2	8×8
5×4	6×2	6×6	7×3	5×5	8×7	3×3	9×8	4×2	0×7
9×4	9×5	8×2	6×4	9×3	5×2	8×4	7×5	5×3	7×6

Problem Solving Answer the question below.

Problem: Each package of balloons contains exactly 4 red balloons, 3 white balloons, and 3 blue balloons. Allen purchased 2 packages of balloons for party decorations. If he wants to use an equal number of each color, what is the greatest number of balloons Allen can use at the party? How many balloons of each color will he use?

Understand

What information am I given?
What am I asked to find or do?

Plan

How can I use the information I am given?
Which strategy should I try?

Solve

Did I follow the plan?
Did I show my work?
Did I write the answer?

Check

Did I use the correct information?
Did I do what was asked?
Is my answer reasonable?

Name ____________________ Time __________

Power-Up Test 9

Use with Lesson 50

Facts Divide.

$7\overline{)49}$	$5\overline{)25}$	$3\overline{)27}$	$3\overline{)24}$	$9\overline{)9}$	$3\overline{)12}$	$4\overline{)16}$	$2\overline{)10}$	$6\overline{)42}$	$4\overline{)28}$
$6\overline{)0}$	$2\overline{)4}$	$5\overline{)35}$	$2\overline{)6}$	$3\overline{)15}$	$6\overline{)54}$	$2\overline{)16}$	$8\overline{)72}$	$5\overline{)30}$	$3\overline{)21}$
$3\overline{)9}$	$9\overline{)81}$	$5\overline{)40}$	$4\overline{)20}$	$7\overline{)56}$	$2\overline{)18}$	$6\overline{)36}$	$8\overline{)56}$	$2\overline{)12}$	$7\overline{)42}$
$6\overline{)48}$	$2\overline{)14}$	$4\overline{)36}$	$4\overline{)24}$	$5\overline{)45}$	$2\overline{)8}$	$3\overline{)18}$	$7\overline{)63}$	$4\overline{)32}$	$8\overline{)64}$

Problem Solving Answer the question below.

Problem: Jessica will roll two dot cubes. She needs to roll a total of 9 on the cubes to win the board game. Copy and complete this table to show the ways Jessica can roll a total of 9 on two dot cubes.

1st Cube	2nd Cube

Understand
What information am I given?
What am I asked to find or do?

Plan
How can I use the information I am given?
Which strategy should I try?

Solve
Did I follow the plan?
Did I show my work?
Did I write the answer?

Check
Did I use the correct information?
Did I do what was asked?
Is my answer reasonable?

Name ______________________ Time __________

Power-Up Test 10

Use with Lesson 55

Facts Multiply.

9 × 6	7 × 1	9 × 2	10 × 10	7 × 4	6 × 5	3 × 2	4 × 4	8 × 6	6 × 3
7 × 7	4 × 3	8 × 5	2 × 2	9 × 9	8 × 3	3 × 0	9 × 7	7 × 2	8 × 8
5 × 4	6 × 2	6 × 6	7 × 3	5 × 5	8 × 7	3 × 3	9 × 8	4 × 2	0 × 7
9 × 4	9 × 5	8 × 2	6 × 4	9 × 3	5 × 2	8 × 4	7 × 5	5 × 3	7 × 6

Problem Solving Answer the question below.

Problem: Ms. Sund will arrange 16 desks into equal-length rows. She will make at least 2 rows, and each row will contain at least 4 desks. How many different arrangements of desks can Ms. Sund make? List or draw the arrangements.

Understand

What information am I given?

What am I asked to find or do?

Plan

How can I use the information I am given?

Which strategy should I try?

Solve

Did I follow the plan?

Did I show my work?

Did I write the answer?

Check

Did I use the correct information?

Did I do what was asked?

Is my answer reasonable?

Name ______________________ Time __________

Power-Up Test 11

Use with Lesson 60

Facts Divide.

$7\overline{)49}$	$5\overline{)25}$	$3\overline{)27}$	$3\overline{)24}$	$9\overline{)9}$	$3\overline{)12}$	$4\overline{)16}$	$2\overline{)10}$	$6\overline{)42}$	$4\overline{)28}$
$6\overline{)0}$	$2\overline{)4}$	$5\overline{)35}$	$2\overline{)6}$	$3\overline{)15}$	$6\overline{)54}$	$2\overline{)16}$	$8\overline{)72}$	$5\overline{)30}$	$3\overline{)21}$
$3\overline{)9}$	$9\overline{)81}$	$5\overline{)40}$	$4\overline{)20}$	$7\overline{)56}$	$2\overline{)18}$	$6\overline{)36}$	$8\overline{)56}$	$2\overline{)12}$	$7\overline{)42}$
$6\overline{)48}$	$2\overline{)14}$	$4\overline{)36}$	$4\overline{)24}$	$5\overline{)45}$	$2\overline{)8}$	$3\overline{)18}$	$7\overline{)63}$	$4\overline{)32}$	$8\overline{)64}$

Problem Solving Answer the question below.

Problem: Shae used a loop of string to form the triangle shown at right. If Shae uses the same loop of string to form a square, what will be the length of each side of the square?

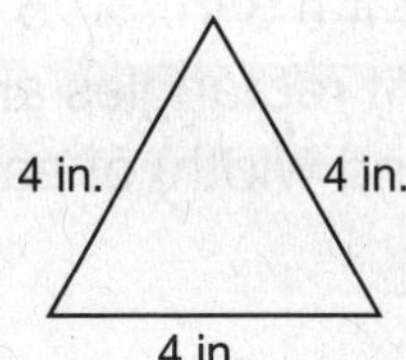

Understand

What information am I given?
What am I asked to find or do?

Plan

How can I use the information I am given?
Which strategy should I try?

Solve

Did I follow the plan?
Did I show my work?
Did I write the answer?

Check

Did I use the correct information?
Did I do what was asked?
Is my answer reasonable?

Name ____________________ Time ______________

Power-Up Test 12

Use with Lesson 65

Facts Divide.

$9\overline{)81}$	$8\overline{)48}$	$6\overline{)18}$	$8\overline{)40}$	$3\overline{)6}$	$7\overline{)28}$	$5\overline{)15}$	$9\overline{)72}$	$7\overline{)14}$	$5\overline{)25}$
$9\overline{)54}$	$8\overline{)32}$	$4\overline{)12}$	$4\overline{)0}$	$6\overline{)12}$	$4\overline{)16}$	$7\overline{)42}$	$2\overline{)4}$	$9\overline{)45}$	$8\overline{)56}$
$8\overline{)24}$	$9\overline{)63}$	$4\overline{)8}$	$5\overline{)20}$	$3\overline{)9}$	$7\overline{)35}$	$9\overline{)36}$	$8\overline{)16}$	$7\overline{)49}$	$8\overline{)8}$
$6\overline{)42}$	$9\overline{)18}$	$6\overline{)30}$	$7\overline{)21}$	$6\overline{)24}$	$5\overline{)10}$	$6\overline{)36}$	$8\overline{)64}$	$9\overline{)27}$	$7\overline{)56}$

Problem Solving Answer the question below.

Problem: If a 3 in. × 5 in. index card is folded as shown, two congruent rectangles are formed. What are the dimensions (length and width) of each rectangle?

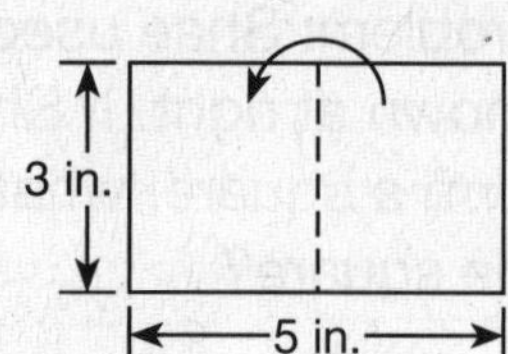

Understand
What information am I given?
What am I asked to find or do?

Plan
How can I use the information I am given?
Which strategy should I try?

Solve
Did I follow the plan?
Did I show my work?
Did I write the answer?

Check
Did I use the correct information?
Did I do what was asked?
Is my answer reasonable?

Name ______________________ Time ____________

Power-Up Test 13

Use with Lesson 70

Facts Divide.

$9\overline{)81}$	$8\overline{)48}$	$6\overline{)18}$	$8\overline{)40}$	$3\overline{)6}$	$7\overline{)28}$	$5\overline{)15}$	$9\overline{)72}$	$7\overline{)14}$	$5\overline{)25}$
$9\overline{)54}$	$8\overline{)32}$	$4\overline{)12}$	$4\overline{)0}$	$6\overline{)12}$	$4\overline{)16}$	$7\overline{)42}$	$2\overline{)4}$	$9\overline{)45}$	$8\overline{)56}$
$8\overline{)24}$	$9\overline{)63}$	$4\overline{)8}$	$5\overline{)20}$	$3\overline{)9}$	$7\overline{)35}$	$9\overline{)36}$	$8\overline{)16}$	$7\overline{)49}$	$8\overline{)8}$
$6\overline{)42}$	$9\overline{)18}$	$6\overline{)30}$	$7\overline{)21}$	$6\overline{)24}$	$5\overline{)10}$	$6\overline{)36}$	$8\overline{)64}$	$9\overline{)27}$	$7\overline{)56}$

Problem Solving Answer the question below.

Problem: Frank, Grey, Hala, and Inez will ride in the same car on the field trip. Three of the children will sit in the back seat of the car. What are the 4 possible combinations of three children? Use the abbreviations F, G, H, and I in your list. (*Hint:* The order of the children does not matter.)

Understand
What information am I given?
What am I asked to find or do?

Plan
How can I use the information I am given?
Which strategy should I try?

Solve
Did I follow the plan?
Did I show my work?
Did I write the answer?

Check
Did I use the correct information?
Did I do what was asked?
Is my answer reasonable?

Name ____________________ Time __________

Power-Up Test 14

Use with Lesson 75

Facts Multiply.

7×9	4×4	2×5	6×9	5×6	3×8	4×9	2×3	7×8	3×5
5×9	3×4	8×9	2×2	10×10	4×6	6×7	2×8	7×7	8×0
8×8	2×7	3×6	5×8	4×7	3×3	9×9	5×7	2×9	7×1
4×5	6×8	2×4	0×0	3×7	4×8	2×6	5×5	3×9	6×6

Problem Solving Answer the question below.

Problem: Martin takes about 500 steps when he walks to the park from his house. In 5 steps, Martin travels about 12 feet. About how many feet does Martin travel when he walks to the park from his house?

Understand

What information am I given?

What am I asked to find or do?

Plan

How can I use the information I am given?

Which strategy should I try?

Solve

Did I follow the plan?

Did I show my work?

Did I write the answer?

Check

Did I use the correct information?

Did I do what was asked?

Is my answer reasonable?

Name ______________________ Time ____________

Facts Multiply.

7×9	4×4	2×5	6×9	5×6	3×8	4×9	2×3	7×8	3×5
5×9	3×4	8×9	2×2	10×10	4×6	6×7	2×8	7×7	8×0
8×8	2×7	3×6	5×8	4×7	3×3	9×9	5×7	2×9	7×1
4×5	6×8	2×4	0×0	3×7	4×8	2×6	5×5	3×9	6×6

Problem Solving Answer the question below.

Problem: Find the missing digits in this multiplication problem.

```
  3_
×  _
----
 3_1
```

Understand

What information am I given?
What am I asked to find or do?

Plan

How can I use the information I am given?
Which strategy should I try?

Solve

Did I follow the plan?
Did I show my work?
Did I write the answer?

Check

Did I use the correct information?
Did I do what was asked?
Is my answer reasonable?

Name ________________ Time __________

Power-Up Test 16

Use with Lesson 85

Facts Multiply.

7 × 9	4 × 4	2 × 5	6 × 9	5 × 6	3 × 8	4 × 9	2 × 3	7 × 8	3 × 5
5 × 9	3 × 4	8 × 9	2 × 2	10 × 10	4 × 6	6 × 7	2 × 8	7 × 7	8 × 0
8 × 8	2 × 7	3 × 6	5 × 8	4 × 7	3 × 3	9 × 9	5 × 7	2 × 9	7 × 1
4 × 5	6 × 8	2 × 4	0 × 0	3 × 7	4 × 8	2 × 6	5 × 5	3 × 9	6 × 6

Problem Solving Answer the question below.

Problem: Henry is covering a 4-by-3 foot bulletin board with black and white construction paper squares, making a checkerboard pattern. Each square is 1 foot by 1 foot. Copy this diagram on your paper, and complete the checkerboard pattern. What is the total area of the bulletin board? How many squares of each color does Henry need?

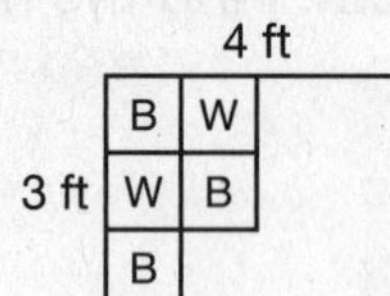

Understand

What information am I given?

What am I asked to find or do?

Plan

How can I use the information I am given?

Which strategy should I try?

Solve

Did I follow the plan?

Did I show my work?

Did I write the answer?

Check

Did I use the correct information?

Did I do what was asked?

Is my answer reasonable?

Name ________________________ Time ____________

Power-Up Test 17

Use with Lesson 90

Facts Write these improper fractions as whole or mixed numbers.

$\frac{8}{3} =$	$\frac{12}{4} =$	$\frac{3}{2} =$	$\frac{4}{3} =$	$\frac{7}{4} =$
$\frac{10}{5} =$	$\frac{10}{9} =$	$\frac{7}{3} =$	$\frac{5}{2} =$	$\frac{11}{8} =$
$\frac{12}{12} =$	$\frac{9}{4} =$	$\frac{12}{5} =$	$\frac{10}{3} =$	$\frac{16}{4} =$
$\frac{13}{5} =$	$\frac{15}{8} =$	$\frac{21}{10} =$	$\frac{9}{2} =$	$\frac{25}{6} =$

Problem Solving Answer the question below.

Problem: Luis built this rectangular prism with small blocks. How many small blocks did he use?

Understand

What information am I given?
What am I asked to find or do?

Plan

How can I use the information I am given?
Which strategy should I try?

Solve

Did I follow the plan?
Did I show my work?
Did I write the answer?

Check

Did I use the correct information?
Did I do what was asked?
Is my answer reasonable?

Name ______________________ Time ____________

Power-Up Test 18

Use with Lesson 95

Facts Divide.

$2\overline{)7}$ R	$3\overline{)16}$ R	$4\overline{)15}$ R	$5\overline{)28}$ R	$4\overline{)21}$ R
$6\overline{)15}$ R	$8\overline{)20}$ R	$2\overline{)15}$ R	$5\overline{)43}$ R	$3\overline{)20}$ R
$6\overline{)27}$ R	$3\overline{)25}$ R	$2\overline{)17}$ R	$3\overline{)10}$ R	$7\overline{)30}$ R
$8\overline{)25}$ R	$3\overline{)8}$ R	$4\overline{)30}$ R	$5\overline{)32}$ R	$7\overline{)50}$ R

Problem Solving Answer the question below.

Problem: List all the possible arrangements of the letters N, O and T.
Bonus: What fraction of the arrangements spell words?

Understand
What information am I given?
What am I asked to find or do?

Plan
How can I use the information I am given?
Which strategy should I try?

Solve
Did I follow the plan?
Did I show my work?
Did I write the answer?

Check
Did I use the correct information?
Did I do what was asked?
Is my answer reasonable?

Name ________________________ Time ____________

Facts

Write these improper fractions as whole or mixed numbers.

$\frac{8}{3} =$	$\frac{12}{4} =$	$\frac{3}{2} =$	$\frac{4}{3} =$	$\frac{7}{4} =$
$\frac{10}{5} =$	$\frac{10}{9} =$	$\frac{7}{3} =$	$\frac{5}{2} =$	$\frac{11}{8} =$
$\frac{12}{12} =$	$\frac{9}{4} =$	$\frac{12}{5} =$	$\frac{10}{3} =$	$\frac{16}{4} =$
$\frac{13}{5} =$	$\frac{15}{8} =$	$\frac{21}{10} =$	$\frac{9}{2} =$	$\frac{25}{6} =$

Problem Solving

Answer the question below.

Problem: Two cups equal a pint. Two pints equal a quart. Two quarts equal a half gallon. Two half gallons equal a gallon. Halle poured 1 cup out of a pitcher that contained a half gallon of lemonade. How many cups of lemonade remained in the pitcher?

Understand

What information am I given?

What am I asked to find or do?

Plan

How can I use the information I am given?

Which strategy should I try?

Solve

Did I follow the plan?

Did I show my work?

Did I write the answer?

Check

Did I use the correct information?

Did I do what was asked?

Is my answer reasonable?

Name ____________________ Time __________

Power-Up Test 20

Use with Lesson 105

Facts Reduce each fraction to lowest terms.

$\frac{2}{10} =$	$\frac{3}{9} =$	$\frac{2}{4} =$	$\frac{6}{8} =$	$\frac{4}{12} =$
$\frac{6}{9} =$	$\frac{4}{8} =$	$\frac{2}{6} =$	$\frac{3}{6} =$	$\frac{6}{10} =$
$\frac{5}{10} =$	$\frac{3}{12} =$	$\frac{2}{8} =$	$\frac{4}{6} =$	$\frac{50}{100} =$
$\frac{2}{12} =$	$\frac{8}{16} =$	$\frac{9}{12} =$	$\frac{25}{100} =$	$\frac{6}{12} =$

Problem Solving Answer the question below.

Problem: The multiples of 7 are 7, 14, 21, 28, and so on. We can use multiples of 7 to count days of the week. For example, 29 days after Tuesday is Wednesday, since 29 days is 4 weeks plus 1 more day. Use the multiples of 7 to find the day of the week that is 68 days after Saturday.

Understand

What information am I given?
What am I asked to find or do?

Plan

How can I use the information I am given?
Which strategy should I try?

Solve

Did I follow the plan?
Did I show my work?
Did I write the answer?

Check

Did I use the correct information?
Did I do what was asked?
Is my answer reasonable?

Name ____________________ Time __________

Power-Up Test 21

Use with Lesson 110

Facts Write these improper fractions as whole or mixed numbers.

$\frac{8}{3}$ =	$\frac{12}{4}$ =	$\frac{3}{2}$ =	$\frac{4}{3}$ =	$\frac{7}{4}$ =
$\frac{10}{5}$ =	$\frac{10}{9}$ =	$\frac{7}{3}$ =	$\frac{5}{2}$ =	$\frac{11}{8}$ =
$\frac{12}{12}$ =	$\frac{9}{4}$ =	$\frac{12}{5}$ =	$\frac{10}{3}$ =	$\frac{16}{4}$ =
$\frac{13}{5}$ =	$\frac{15}{8}$ =	$\frac{21}{10}$ =	$\frac{9}{2}$ =	$\frac{25}{6}$ =

Problem Solving Answer the question below.

Problem: Reggie scored 5 points in the first game and 9 points in the second game. How many points does Reggie need in the third game to achieve an average of 8 points per game?

Understand

What information am I given?
What am I asked to find or do?

Plan

How can I use the information I am given?
Which strategy should I try?

Solve

Did I follow the plan?
Did I show my work?
Did I write the answer?

Check

Did I use the correct information?
Did I do what was asked?
Is my answer reasonable?

Name ______________________ Time __________

Use with Lesson 115

Facts Simplify.

$\frac{6}{4} =$	$\frac{10}{8} =$	$\frac{9}{12} =$	$\frac{12}{9} =$	$\frac{12}{10} =$
$\frac{12}{8} =$	$\frac{8}{6} =$	$\frac{10}{4} =$	$\frac{8}{20} =$	$\frac{20}{8} =$
$\frac{24}{6} =$	$\frac{9}{6} =$	$\frac{15}{10} =$	$\frac{8}{12} =$	$\frac{10}{6} =$
$\frac{16}{10} =$	$\frac{9}{12} =$	$\frac{15}{6} =$	$\frac{10}{20} =$	$\frac{18}{12} =$

Problem Solving Answer the question below.

Problem: Sandi will spin this spinner three times and write the result after each spin. List all the possible outcomes that Sandi could get with three spins. Make a tree diagram to help you find the outcomes.

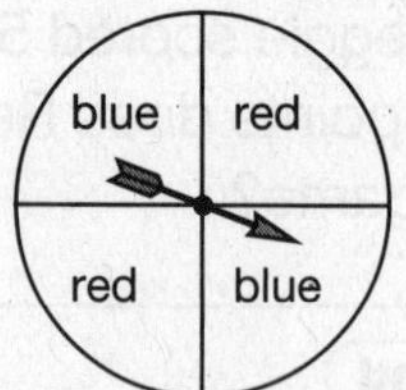

Understand

What information am I given?
What am I asked to find or do?

Plan

How can I use the information I am given?
Which strategy should I try?

Solve

Did I follow the plan?
Did I show my work?
Did I write the answer?

Check

Did I use the correct information?
Did I do what was asked?
Is my answer reasonable?

Name ______________________ Time ____________

Power-Up Test 23

Use with Lesson 120

Facts Reduce each fraction to lowest terms.

$\frac{2}{10}$ =	$\frac{3}{9}$ =	$\frac{2}{4}$ =	$\frac{6}{8}$ =	$\frac{4}{12}$ =
$\frac{6}{9}$ =	$\frac{4}{8}$ =	$\frac{2}{6}$ =	$\frac{3}{6}$ =	$\frac{6}{10}$ =
$\frac{5}{10}$ =	$\frac{3}{12}$ =	$\frac{2}{8}$ =	$\frac{4}{6}$ =	$\frac{50}{100}$ =
$\frac{2}{12}$ =	$\frac{8}{16}$ =	$\frac{9}{12}$ =	$\frac{25}{100}$ =	$\frac{6}{12}$ =

Problem Solving Answer the question below.

Problem: How many 1-inch cubes would be needed to build a rectangular solid 4 inches long, 3 inches wide, and 2 inches high?

2 in.

3 in.

4 in.

Understand
What information am I given?
What am I asked to find or do?

Plan
How can I use the information I am given?
Which strategy should I try?

Solve
Did I follow the plan?
Did I show my work?
Did I write the answer?

Check
Did I use the correct information?
Did I do what was asked?
Is my answer reasonable?

Name ____________________

Score ____________________

Cumulative Test 1A

Also take **Power-Up Test 1**

Write the next three terms in each counting sequence for problems **1–3.**

1. (1) 7, 14, 21, 28, _____, _____, _____, ...

2. (1) 24, 32, 40, 48, _____, _____, _____, ...

3. (1) 36, 32, 28, 24, _____, _____, _____, ...

4. (1) What is the last digit of 85,236?

5. (2) If a whole number is not odd, then it is what?

6. (2) Which of these numbers is odd?

A. 6789 **B.** 9876 **C.** 7968

7. (2) Which of these numbers is even?

A. 5647 **B.** 4576 **C.** 6745

8. (2) In the basket there is one more orange than there are pears. Which of the following could not be the total number of oranges and pears in the basket?

A. 44 **B.** 43 **C.** 45

9. (3) Use digits to write the number for "8 hundreds plus 2 tens plus 3 ones."

10. (3) Which digit in 719 shows the number of tens?

11. (3) How much is 2 hundreds plus 9 tens?

12. What number equals 10 tens?
(3)

For problems **13** and **14**, write each comparison using digits and a comparison symbol.

13. Forty is greater than fourteen.
(4)

14. Seventeen is less than twenty.
(4)

15. Compare: 321 ◯ 199
(4)

16. Compare: 53 ◯ 45
(4)

17. Use words to name $319.45.
(5)

18. Use words to name 409.
(5)

19. Use digits to write six hundred thirteen dollars and eighty cents.
(5)

20. Use digits to write seven hundred ninety-six.
(5)

Name ______________________________

Score ______________________________

Cumulative Test 1B

Also take **Power-Up Test 1**

Write the next three terms in each counting sequence for problems **1–3**.

1. (1) 6, 12, 18, 24, _____, _____, _____, ...

2. (1) 81, 72, 63, 54, _____, _____, _____, ...

3. (1) 18, 21, 24, 27, _____, _____, _____, ...

4. (1) What is the last digit of 36,274?

5. (2) If a whole number is not even, then it is what?

6. (2) Which of these numbers is even?

A. 3542 **B.** 2543 **C.** 4325

7. (2) Which of these numbers is odd?

A. 1234 **B.** 3412 **C.** 2341

8. (2) In the kennel there is one more dog than there are cats. Which of the following could not be the total number of dogs and cats in the kennel?

A. 31 **B.** 30 **C.** 29

9. (3) Use digits to write the number for "5 hundreds plus 3 tens plus 7 ones."

10. (3) Which digit in 365 shows the number of tens?

11. (3) How much is 4 hundreds plus 5 tens?

12. (3) How many tens equal one hundred?

For problems **13** and **14**, write each comparison using digits and a comparison symbol.

13. (4) Fifteen is less than fifty.

14. (4) Twelve is greater than ten.

15. (4) Compare: 101 ◯ 110

16. (4) Compare: 54 ◯ 45

17. (5) Use words to name $253.15.

18. (5) Use words to name 102.

19. (5) Use digits to write four hundred forty dollars and fourteen cents.

20. (5) Use digits to write two hundred five.

Name ______________________________

Score ______________________________

Cumulative Test 2A

Also take **Power-Up Test 2**

1. (11) In Mako's pasture there are seventeen horses and eighteen buffalo. Altogether, how many horses and buffalo are in his pasture?

2. (2) Celeste worked in her garden for 40 minutes. She spent half the time working in the rose bed. How many minutes did Celeste spend working in the rose bed?

3. (8) For the fact family 3, 4, and 7, write two addition facts and two subtraction facts.

4. (7) Use digits to write two hundred eleven thousand, five hundred six.

5. (2) Use the three digits 3, 4, and 5 once each to make an odd number greater than 500.

Find each missing addend in problems **6** and **7**.

6. (10) $13 + r = 21$

7. (10) $c + 24 = 51$

8. (3) Which digit in 43,987 shows the number of hundreds?

9. (4, 8) Compare: $37 - 7 \bigcirc 38 - 8$

10. (2) Think of two odd numbers. Subtract the smaller from the larger. Is the difference odd or even?

11. (7) Nadine is third in line. Roland is eighth in the same line. How many people are between them?

12. (6)
$$\begin{array}{r} 381 \\ 46 \\ +\ 173 \\ \hline \end{array}$$

13. (9)
$$\begin{array}{r} 716 \\ -\ 208 \\ \hline \end{array}$$

14. (9)
$$\begin{array}{r} 700 \\ -\ 328 \\ \hline \end{array}$$

15. (6)
$$\begin{array}{r} 5 \\ 9 \\ 5 \\ 3 \\ +\ 1 \\ \hline \end{array}$$

16. (9) $207 − $80

17. (6) $52 + $208 + $7

Write the next term in each counting sequence for problems **18–20**.

18. (1) 6, 12, 18, _____, ...

19. (1) 25, 30, 35, _____, ...

20. (1) 64, 56, 48, _____, ...

Name ______________________________

Score ______________________________

Cumulative Test 2B

Also take ***Power-Up Test 2***

1. (11) In Tom's class there are fifteen boys and sixteen girls. Altogether, how many boys and girls are in his class?

2. (2) In Jane's class there are 30 students. Half the students are girls. How many girls are in Jane's class?

3. (8) For the fact family 4, 6, and 10, write two addition facts and two subtraction facts.

4. (7) Use digits to write four hundred eight thousand, nine hundred eleven.

5. (2) Use the three digits 1, 2, and 3 once each to make an even number greater than 200.

Find each missing addend in problems **6** and **7.**

6. (10) $12 + m = 21$

7. (10) $a + 16 = 40$

8. (3) Which digit in 38,425 shows the number of hundreds?

9. (4, 8) Compare: 25 − 5 ◯ 26 − 6

10. (2) Think of two odd numbers. Add them together. Is the sum odd or even?

11. (7) Vada is fifth in line. Keenan is twelfth in the same line. How many people are between them?

12. (6)

$$\begin{array}{r} 562 \\ 27 \\ +\ 181 \\ \hline \end{array}$$

13. (9)

$$\begin{array}{r} 764 \\ -\ 158 \\ \hline \end{array}$$

14. (9)

$$\begin{array}{r} 600 \\ -\ 146 \\ \hline \end{array}$$

15. (6)

$$\begin{array}{r} 6 \\ 8 \\ 3 \\ 4 \\ +\ 7 \\ \hline \end{array}$$

16. (9) \$143 − \$60

17. (6) \$42 + \$163 + \$8

Write the next term in each counting sequence for problems **18–20.**

18. (1) 7, 14, 21, _____, ...

19. (1) 30, 40, 50, _____, ...

20. (1) 63, 54, 45, _____, ...

Name ______________________________

Score ______________________________

Cumulative Test 3A

Also take **Power-Up Test 3**

1. (8) Write two addition facts and two subtraction facts for the fact family 9, 8, and 17.

2. (15) What is the product of 4 and 7?

3. (12) Draw a number line marked with the integers from −6 to 6.

4. (12) Which figure shows a segment?

A. •————•

B. •————→

C. ←————→

5. (14) Find the missing number:

$$10 - s = 3$$

6. (11) There are 24 minnows and 11 guppies in the fish tank. Altogether, how many minnows and guppies are in the fish tank?

7. (11) Beth ate 17 strawberries before noon. If she ate 32 strawberries all day, how many strawberries did Beth eat after noon?

8. (12) Use tally marks to show the number thirteen.

9. (15) Which number sentence illustrates the Identity Property of Multiplication?

A. $5 \times 2 = 2 \times 5$

B. $5 \times 0 = 0$

C. $5 \times 1 = 5$

10. (13) Change this addition problem to a multiplication problem:

8 + 8 + 8 + 8

11. (9) 316 − 48

12. (13)
```
   $2.91
   $4.69
 + $8.03
```

13. (6)
```
   742
    27
 + 840
```

14. (13)
```
   $6.28
 − $4.56
```

15. (9)
```
   800
 − 335
```

16. (7) Which digit is in the ten-thousands place in 406,291?

17. (7) Use digits to write the number six hundred eleven thousand, two hundred four.

18. (15) How much is 3 nines?

19. (7) Compare: 2442 ◯ 2424

20. (1) What is the **seventh** term in this counting sequence?

6, 12, 18, 24, ...

Name ______________________

Score ______________________

Cumulative Test 3B

Also take **Power-Up Test 3**

1. (8) Write two addition facts and two subtraction facts for the fact family 7, 8, and 15.

2. (15) What is the product of 6 and 3?

3. (12) Draw a number line marked with the integers from –5 to 5.

4. (12) Which figure shows a segment?

A. ⟷

B. ⟶

C. ——

5. (14) Find the missing number:

$10 - m = 4$

6. (11) There are 16 boys and 13 girls in the class. Altogether, how many boys and girls are in the class?

7. (11) Chucho scored 13 points in the first half of the game. If he scored 22 points in the whole game, how many points did Chucho score in the second half?

8. (12) Use tally marks to show the number eleven.

9. (15) Which number sentence illustrates the Identity Property of Multiplication?

A. $3 \times 4 = 4 \times 3$

B. $4 \times 1 = 4$

C. $4 \times 0 = 0$

10. (13) Change this addition problem to a multiplication problem:

$6 + 6 + 6 + 6 + 6$

11. (9) $203 - 56$

12. (13)

$$\begin{array}{r} \$4.16 \\ \$2.18 \\ + \$1.84 \\ \hline \end{array}$$

13. (6)

$$\begin{array}{r} 621 \\ 75 \\ + 960 \\ \hline \end{array}$$

14. (13)

$$\begin{array}{r} \$4.13 \\ - \$3.45 \\ \hline \end{array}$$

15. (9)

$$\begin{array}{r} 700 \\ - 345 \\ \hline \end{array}$$

16. (7) Which digit is in the tens place in 529,674?

17. (7) Use digits to write the number twenty-one thousand, three hundred fifty.

18. (15) How much is 4 sevens?

19. (7) Compare: 1323 ◯ 1332

20. (1) What is the **eighth** term in this counting sequence?

7, 14, 21, 28, ...

Name ______________________________

Score ______________________________

Cumulative Test 4A

Also take ***Power-Up Test 4***

1. (11) Daniel cleaned 2 sofas. In one he found 125 coins. In the other he found 226 coins. How many coins did Daniel find in both sofas combined?

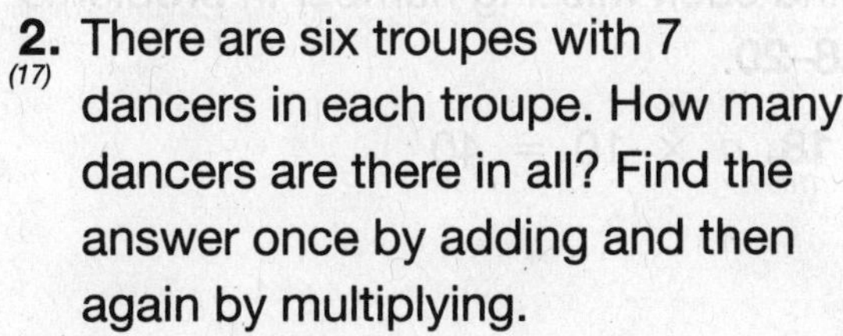

2. (17) There are six troupes with 7 dancers in each troupe. How many dancers are there in all? Find the answer once by adding and then again by multiplying.

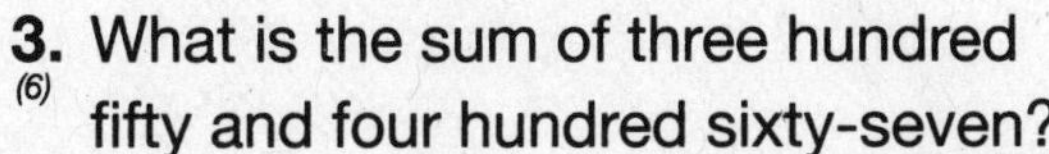

3. (6) What is the sum of three hundred fifty and four hundred sixty-seven?

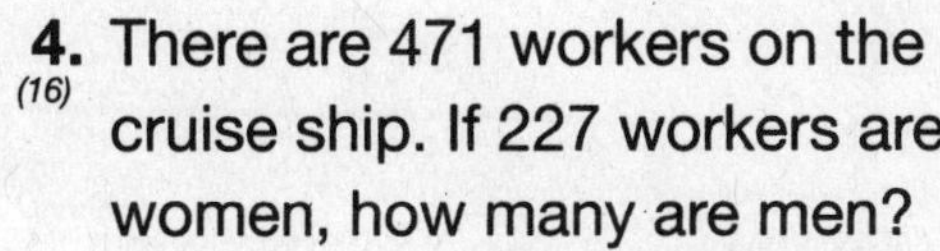

4. (16) There are 471 workers on the cruise ship. If 227 workers are women, how many are men?

5. (12) Use tally marks to show the number nine.

6. (12) Compare: $-5 \bigcirc 5$

7. (13) Compare:
$7 + 7 + 7 + 7 \bigcirc 7 \times 5$

8. (12) Which of these lines is vertical?

A. ⟷

B.

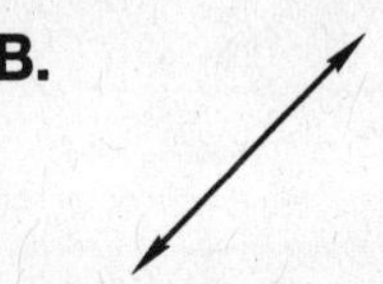

C.

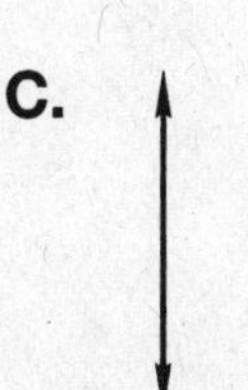

9. (2, 15) Think of two even numbers. Multiply them. Is the product odd or even?

10. (17)
$$\begin{array}{r} \$21 \\ \times \quad 7 \\ \hline \end{array}$$

11. (17)
$$\begin{array}{r} \$2.92 \\ \times \quad 3 \\ \hline \end{array}$$

12. (9)
$$\begin{array}{r} 5492 \\ -\ 4817 \\ \hline \end{array}$$

13. (13)
$$\begin{array}{r} \$40.00 \\ -\ \$11.92 \\ \hline \end{array}$$

14. (18) $9 \times 2 \times 4$

15. (20) $7\overline{)35}$

16. (20) $18 \div 2$

17. (20) $\frac{36}{6}$

Find each missing number in problems 18–20.

18. (18) $n \times 10 = 40$

19. (14) $m - 28 = 54$

20. (10) $312 + e = 538$

Name ______________________________

Score ______________________________

Cumulative

Also take **Power-Up**

1. (11) Elizabeth read 2 books. One book had 288 pages. The other had 306 pages. How many pages did Elizabeth read in all?

2. (17) There are four teams with 8 players on each team. How many players are there in all? Find the answer once by adding and then again by multiplying.

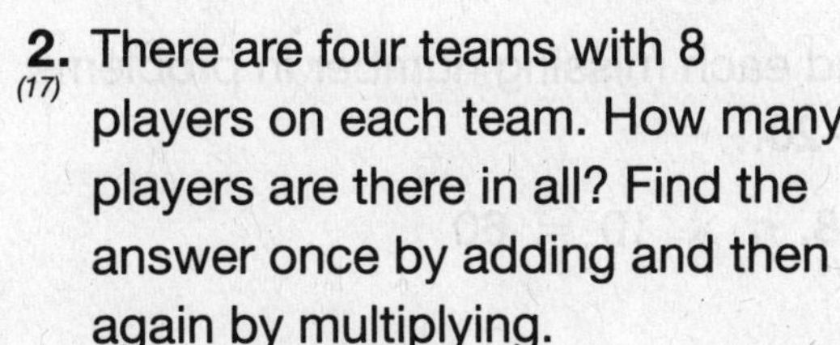

3. (6) What is the sum of two hundred ninety and three hundred nineteen?

4. (16) There are 523 students at Rio Vista School. If 284 students are girls, how many are boys?

5. (12) Use tally marks to show the number seven.

6. (12) Compare: $-3 \bigcirc 3$

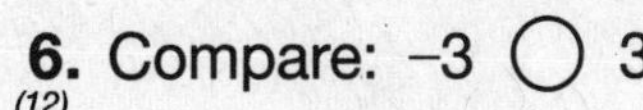

7. (13) Compare:
$6 + 6 + 6 + 6 + 6 \bigcirc 4 \times 6$

8. (12) Which of these lines is horizontal?

A. ⟷

B.

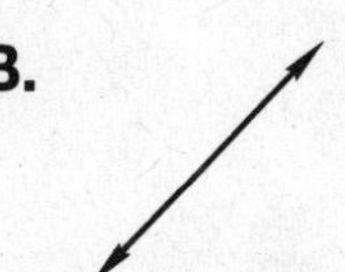

C.

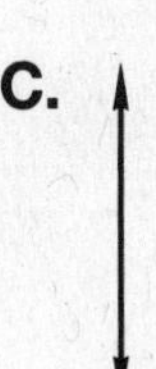

9. (2, 15) Think of two odd numbers. Multiply them. Is the product odd or even?

10. (17)
$$\begin{array}{r} \$43 \\ \times \quad 5 \\ \hline \end{array}$$

11. (17) $\$3.06 \times 4$

12. (9) $3146 - 1427$

13. (13) $\$30.00 - \$14.73$

14. (18) $3 \times 4 \times 5$

15. (20) $6\overline{)24}$

16. (20) $24 \div 8$

17. (20) $\frac{24}{4}$

Find each missing number in problems **18–20.**

18. (18) $n \times 10 = 60$

19. (14) $n - 36 = 45$

20. (10) $225 + n = 419$

Name ______________________________

Score ______________________________

Cumulative Test 5A

Also take ***Power-Up Test 5***

1. List the factors of 16.
(25)

2. Sylvester lined up the 42 cans in 6 equal rows. How many cans were in each row?
(21)

Use the following information to answer problems **3** and **4**:

In Mr. Hardin's class, one tenth of the 20 students play football. One fourth of the students play baseball, and one half of the students play soccer.

3. How many students play soccer?
(Inv. 2)

4. How many students play baseball?
(Inv. 2)

5. Write two multiplication facts and two division facts for the fact family 3, 7, and 21.
(19)

6. What is the sum of eight hundred fourteen and four hundred eight?
(6)

7. On the shelf there are 3 rows of mugs. If each row has 8 mugs in it, how many mugs are there?
(21)

8. Compare:
(24)
$(4 \times 3) + 2 \bigcirc 4 \times (3 + 2)$

9. Which fraction is not equal to $\frac{1}{2}$?
(23)

A. $\frac{2}{4}$ **B.** $\frac{5}{10}$ **C.** $\frac{7}{15}$ **D.** $\frac{50}{100}$

10. $7 + $3.50 + $0.75
(13)

11. $6 − $3.28
(13)

12. (24) $16 \div (8 \div 2)$

13. (22) $8\overline{)58}$

14. (20) $\frac{54}{9}$

15. (17)

$$\begin{array}{r} \$5.13 \\ \times \quad 9 \\ \hline \end{array}$$

16. (18) $8 \times 7 \times 10$

17. (17) 908×3

18. (6)

$$\begin{array}{r} 3621 \\ 405 \\ +\ 1037 \\ \hline \end{array}$$

19. (9)

$$\begin{array}{r} 2000 \\ -\ 321 \\ \hline \end{array}$$

20. (24) Which number sentence below illustrates the Associative Property of Multiplication?

A. $3 \times 4 = 4 \times 3$

B. $3 \times 1 = 3$

C. $3 \times (4 \times 5) = (3 \times 4) \times 5$

Name ______________________

Score ______________________

Cumulative Test 5B

Also take **Power-Up Test 5**

1. (25) List the factors of 18.

2. (21) The 28 students lined up in 4 equal rows. How many students were in each row?

Use the following information to answer problems **3** and **4**:

In Mrs. Abita's class, one fourth of the 20 students play football. One half of the students play baseball, and one tenth of the students play soccer.

3. (Inv. 2) How many students play football?

4. (Inv. 2) How many students play soccer?

5. (19) Write two multiplication facts and two division facts for the fact family 4, 5, and 20.

6. (6) What is the sum of nine hundred sixty and six hundred nineteen?

7. (21) In the classroom there are 4 rows of desks. If each row has 7 desks in it, how many desks are there?

8. (24) Compare:
$2 \times (3 + 4) \bigcirc (2 \times 3) + 4$

9. (23) Which fraction is not equal to $\frac{1}{2}$?

A. $\frac{4}{8}$ **B.** $\frac{12}{25}$ **C.** $\frac{25}{50}$ **D.** $\frac{100}{200}$

10. (13) $10 + $6.75 + $0.75

11. (13) $5 − $2.63

12. $12 \div (6 \div 2)$
(24)

13. $9\overline{)60}$
(22)

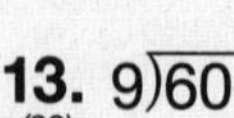

14. $\frac{36}{4}$
(20)

15. $\begin{array}{r} \$3.08 \\ \times \quad 7 \\ \hline \end{array}$
(17)

16. $10 \times 8 \times 6$
(18)

17. 368×4
(17)

18. $\begin{array}{r} 4534 \\ 273 \\ +\ 1089 \\ \hline \end{array}$
(6)

19. $\begin{array}{r} 1000 \\ -\ 76 \\ \hline \end{array}$
(9)

20. Which number sentence below illustrates the Associative Property of Addition?
(24)

A. $2 + (3 + 4) = (2 + 3) + 4$

B. $2 + 3 = 3 + 2$

C. $2 + 0 = 2$

Name ______________________________

Score ______________________________

Cumulative Test 6A

Also take **Power-Up Test 6**

1. Six centuries is how many years?
(28)

2. Coletta bought four fruit bars for $1.05 each and 2 drinks for $0.90 each. How much did she spend in all?
(13)

3. What is the product of seventeen and six?
(17)

4. Xavier, Camille, Tori, and Rosalina equally shared 32 ounces of fruit juice. How many ounces of fruit juice did each person drink?
(21)

5. What is the largest three-digit even number that uses the digits 3, 4, and 5?
(2)

6. Think of an even number. Multiply it by 3. Is the product odd or even?
(2)

7. If Giancarlo is sixth in line, how many people are in front of him?
(7)

8. What temperature is shown on this thermometer?
(27)

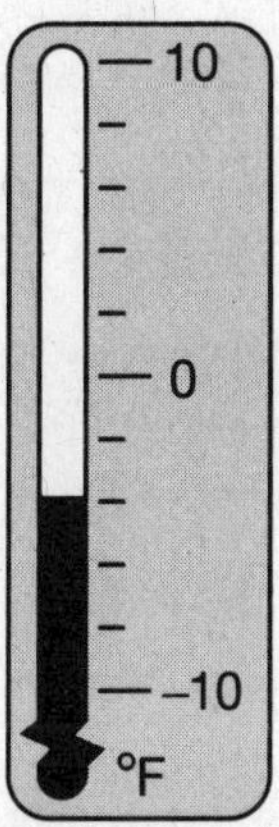

9. List the factors of 24.
(25)

10. (9)

$$\begin{array}{r} 2694 \\ -\ 1086 \\ \hline \end{array}$$

11. (13)

$$\begin{array}{r} \$40.00 \\ -\ \$\ 8.21 \\ \hline \end{array}$$

12. (6)

$$\begin{array}{r} 26 \\ 61 \\ 8 \\ 67 \\ +\ 13 \\ \hline \end{array}$$

13. (26) $482 \div 5$

14. (26, 20) $\dfrac{300}{6}$

15. (26) $9\overline{)\$4.59}$

16. (29) 20×87

17. (24) $7 \times (3 + 9)$

18. (17)

$$\begin{array}{r} \$4.92 \\ \times\ \ \ \ 4 \\ \hline \end{array}$$

19. (23) Compare: $\frac{1}{2} \bigcirc \frac{3}{8}$

20. (28) If it is evening, what time is shown by this clock?

Name ______________________________

Score ______________________________

Cumulative Test 6B

Also take ***Power-Up Test 6***

1. Four decades is how many years?
(28)

2. Jeremy bought two sandwiches for $1.35 each and a drink for $0.90. How much did he spend in all?
(13)

3. What is the product of eighteen and eight?
(17)

4. Imani, Vera, Debbie, and Steve equally shared a dozen pencils. How many pencils did each person get?
(21)

5. What is the largest three-digit odd number that uses the digits 6, 7, and 8?
(2)

6. Think of an odd number. Multiply it by 2. Is the product odd or even?
(2)

7. If Letha is fourth in line, how many people are in front of her?
(7)

8. What temperature is shown on this thermometer?
(27)

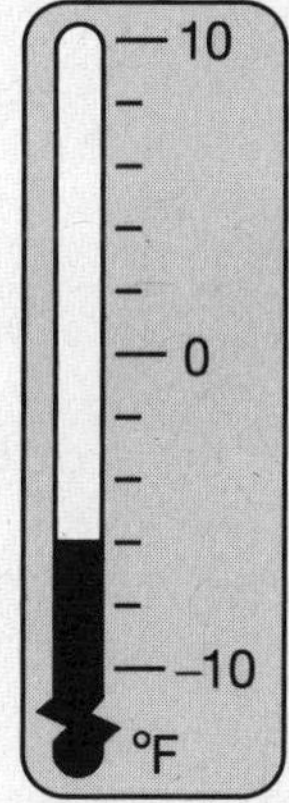

9. List the factors of 32.
(25)

10. (9)
$$\begin{array}{r} 3453 \\ -\ 1647 \\ \hline \end{array}$$

11. (13)
$$\begin{array}{r} \$30.00 \\ -\ \$\ 6.42 \\ \hline \end{array}$$

12. (6)
$$\begin{array}{r} 32 \\ 54 \\ 18 \\ 76 \\ +\ 5 \\ \hline \end{array}$$

13. (26) $397 \div 6$

14. (26) $\frac{300}{4}$

15. (26) $8\overline{)\$9.68}$

16. (29) 30×45

17. (24) $6 \times (7 + 8)$

18. (17)
$$\begin{array}{r} \$3.56 \\ \times\quad 7 \\ \hline \end{array}$$

19. (23) Compare: $\frac{1}{2} \bigcirc \frac{5}{12}$

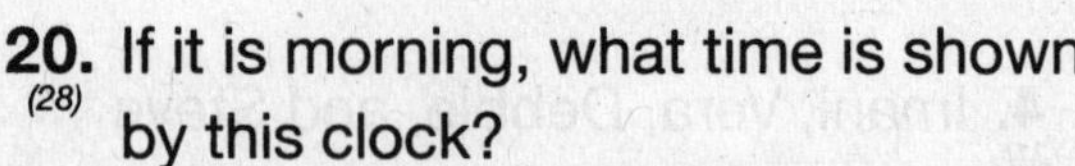

20. (28) If it is morning, what time is shown by this clock?

Name ______________________________

Score ______________________________

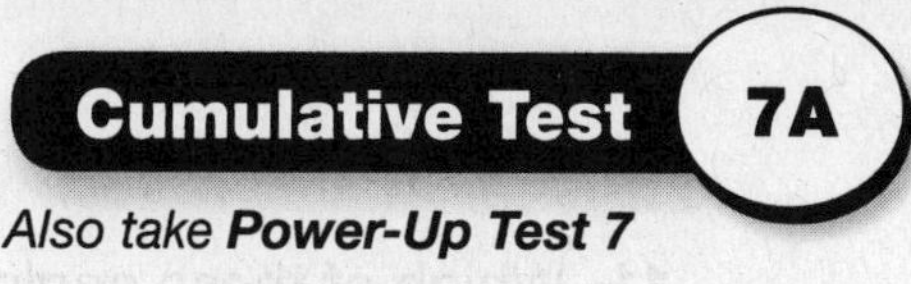

Also take ***Power-Up Test 7***

1. (31) Draw a pair of parallel lines that are oblique.

2. (28) If it is early morning, what time is shown by this clock?

3. (35) How many years were there from 1864 to 1895?

4. (25) List the factors of 15.

5. (21) The Albans drink 12 gallons of milk each week. Four quarts equals one gallon. How many quarts of milk do the Albans drink each week?

6. (33) Round 57 to the nearest ten.

7. (33) Round 804 to the nearest hundred.

8. (24) Compare:
$15 - (10 + 5) \bigcirc (15 - 10) + 5$

9. (30) What fraction of the square is shaded?

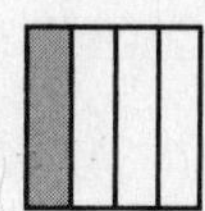

10. (30) What percent of the square is shaded?

11. Which of these angles is an obtuse angle?
(31)

A. 

B. 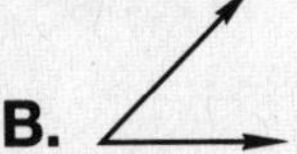

C. 

12. The arrow is pointing to what number on this number line?
(27)

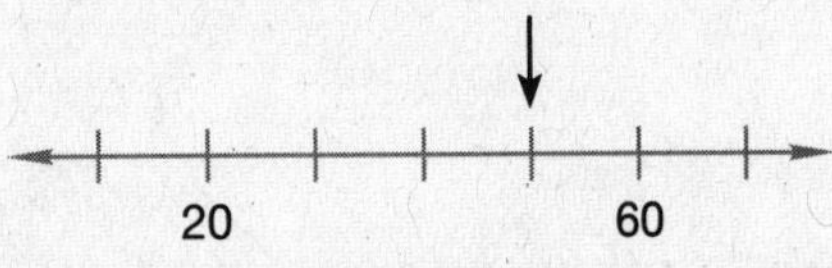

13. \$4.82 + \$13 + \$0.64
(13)

14. \$20 − \$13.80
(13)

15. $7 \times 13 \times 30$
(18)

16. \$2.75 × 20
(29)

17. $7\overline{)4928}$
(34)

18. $291 \div 4$
(26)

19. $\frac{2000}{8}$
(34)

20. Which figure is not a polygon?
(32)

A. 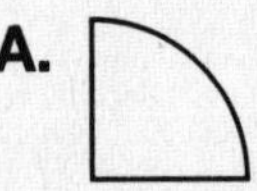

B.

C. 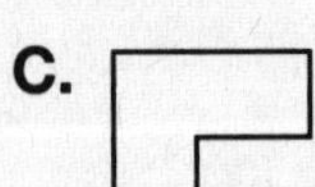

D.

Name ______________________________

Score ______________________________

Cumulative Test 7B

Also take **Power-Up Test 8**

1. Draw a pair of parallel lines that are horizontal.
(31)

2. If it is evening, what time is shown by this clock?
(28)

3. How many years were there from 1902 to 1969?
(35)

4. List the factors of 21.
(25)

5. The gas tank in Mario's car holds 16 gallons of gas. Four quarts equals one gallon. How many quarts of gas does Mario's gas tank hold?
(21)

6. Round 83 to the nearest ten.
(33)

7. Round 582 to the nearest hundred.
(33)

8. Compare:
(24)

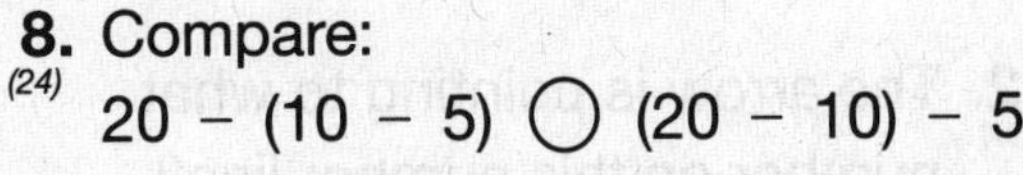

20 − (10 − 5) ○ (20 − 10) − 5

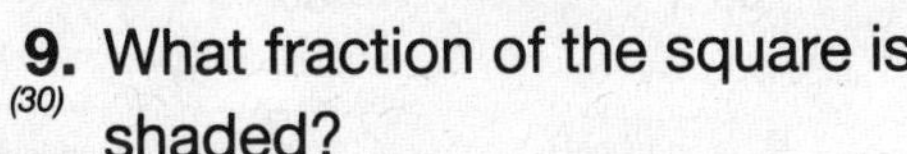

9. What fraction of the square is shaded?
(30)

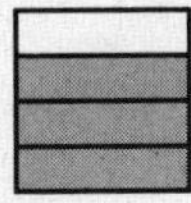

10. What percent of the square is shaded?
(30)

11. Which of these angles is a right angle?
(31)

A. 

B. 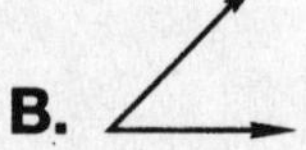

C. 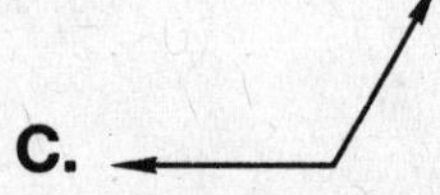

12. The arrow is pointing to what number on this number line?
(27)

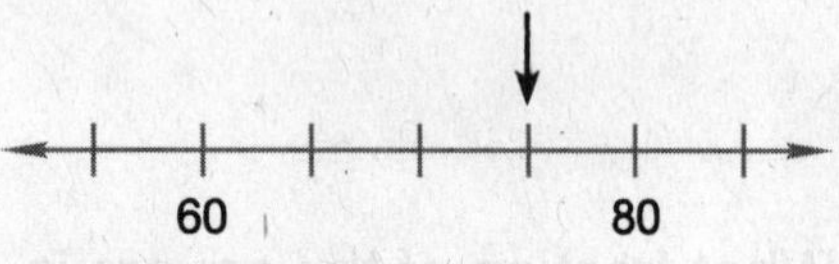

13. \$6.57 + \$12 + \$0.79
(13)

14. \$10 − \$6.45
(13)

15. $8 \times 12 \times 20$
(18)

16. \$1.25 × 40
(29)

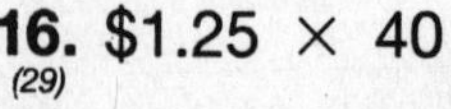

17. $8\overline{)4864}$
(34)

18. $368 \div 5$
(26)

19. $\frac{3000}{6}$
(34)

20. Which figure is not a polygon?
(32)

A. 

B. 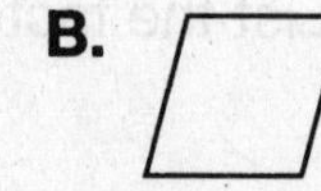

C. 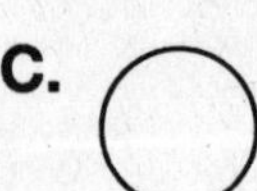

D.

Name ______________________________

Score ______________________________

Cumulative Test 8A

Also take ***Power-Up Test 8***

1. (35) There are 13 more orchids than azaleas. If there are 26 azaleas, how many orchids are there?

2. (38) To what mixed number is the arrow pointing?

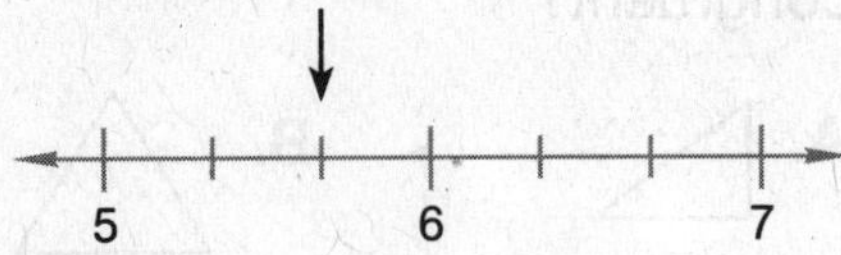

3. (32) Which of these figures is a pentagon?

A.  **B.** 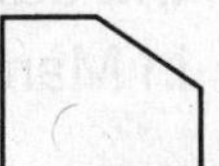

C. 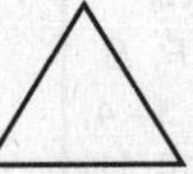 **D.** 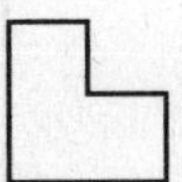

4. (36) Draw an isosceles triangle.

5. (39) Compare these fractions. Draw and shade two congruent circles to show the comparison.

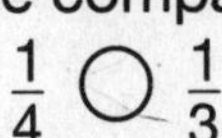

$\frac{1}{4} \bigcirc \frac{1}{3}$

6. (33) Round 758 to the nearest hundred.

7. (27) What temperature is shown on this thermometer?

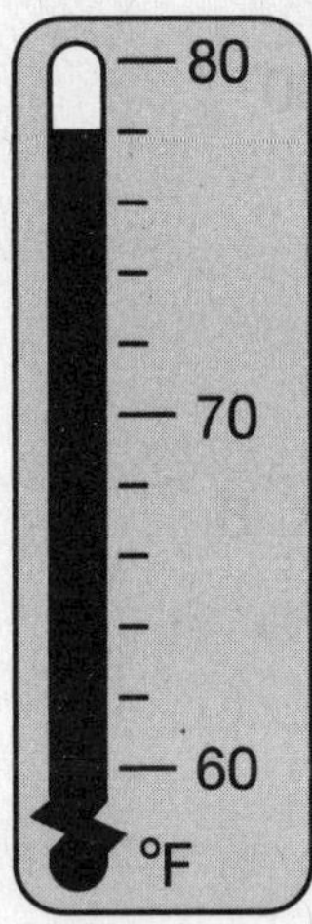

8. (11) When Arthur finished page 98 of a 230-page book, he still had how many pages to read?

9. (30) What fraction of this group of circles is shaded?

10. $802 + $0.92 + $4.79
(13)

11. 4803 − 2166
(9)

12. 621 × 200
(29)

13. 5 × 14 × 8
(18)

14. $7\overline{)\$7.63}$
(34)

15. $\frac{546}{6}$
(26)

16. 242 ÷ 3
(34)

17. $90 − $46.55
(13)

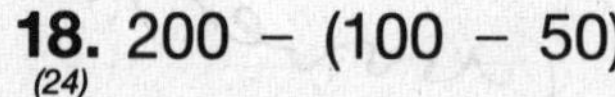

18. 200 − (100 − 50)
(24)

19. Which two triangles below are congruent?
(32)

A.

B.

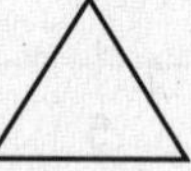

C.

D.

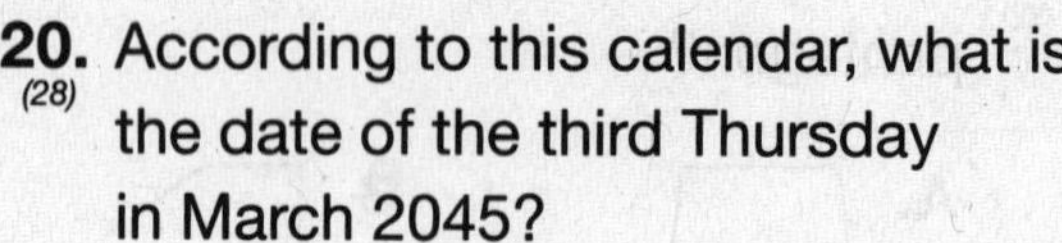

20. According to this calendar, what is the date of the third Thursday in March 2045?
(28)

March 2045

S	M	T	W	T	F	S
			1	2	3	4
5	6	7	8	9	10	11
12	13	14	15	16	17	18
19	20	21	22	23	24	25
26	27	28	29	30	31	

Name ______________________

Score ______________________

Cumulative Test 8B

Also take **Power-Up Test 8**

1. (35) There are 7 more runners than walkers. If there are 11 walkers, how many runners are there?

2. (38) To what mixed number is the arrow pointing?

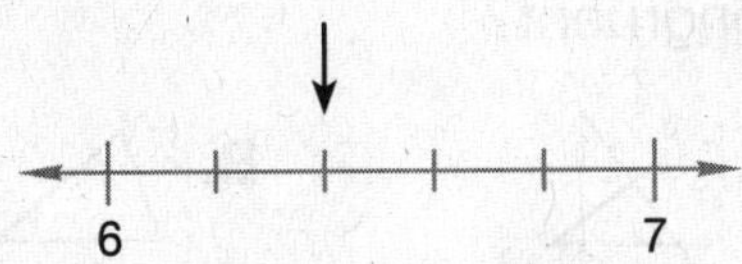

3. (32) Which of these figures is a quadrilateral?

A. 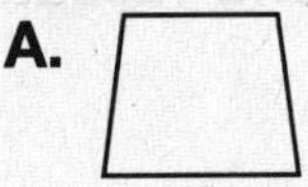 **B.** 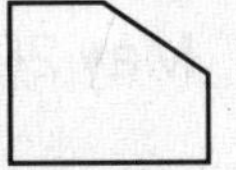

C. 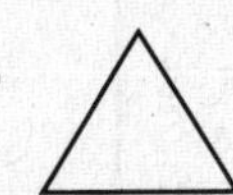 **D.** 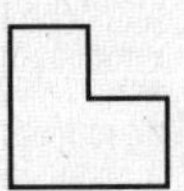

4. (36) Draw an equilateral triangle.

5. (39) Compare these fractions. Draw and shade two congruent circles to show the comparison.

$\frac{1}{2} \bigcirc \frac{1}{2}$

6. (33) Round 632 to the nearest hundred.

7. (27) What temperature is shown on this thermometer?

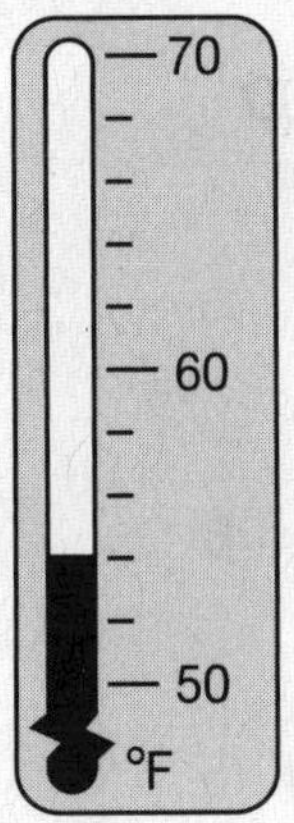

8. (11) When Sumiko finished page 129 of a 320-page book, she still had how many pages to read?

9. (30) What fraction of this group of circles is shaded?

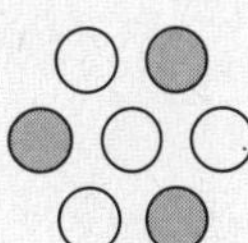

10. $526 + $0.37 + $4.60
(13)

11. 3726 − 1654
(9)

12. 345 × 300
(29)

13. 5 × 12 × 6
(18)

14. $5\overline{)\$5.35}$
(34)

15. $\frac{424}{8}$
(26)

16. 363 ÷ 4
(34)

17. $100 − $35.40
(13)

18. 100 − (10 − 1)
(24)

19. Which two triangles below are congruent?
(32)

A. **B.**

C. **D.**

20. According to this calendar, what is the date of the second Tuesday in May 2024?
(28)

May 2024

S	M	T	W	T	F	S
			1	2	3	4
5	6	7	8	9	10	11
12	13	14	15	16	17	18
19	20	21	22	23	24	25
26	27	28	29	30	31	

Name ______________________________

Score ______________________________

Cumulative Test 9A

Also take ***Power-Up Test 9***

Refer to this function table to answer problems **1** and **2**:

In	2	6	12
Out	1	3	6

1. (Inv. 4) What does the function do to each "in" number?

A. It subtracts 9.

B. It divides by 2.

C. It divides by 4.

D. It multiplies by 2.

2. (Inv. 4) If 8 is used as the "in" number, what will be the "out" number?

3. (44) Use an inch ruler to measure the length of this segment to the nearest eighth of an inch:

4. (43) What mixed number is half of 45?

5. (45) Which of the quadrilaterals below is not a parallelogram?

A. 

B.

C.

D. 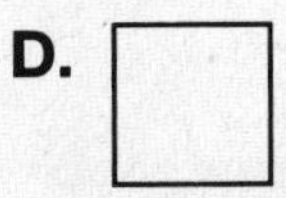

6. (40) What mixed number names the number of shaded circles shown below?

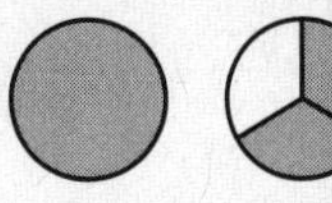

7. (44) A key that is 60 millimeters long is how many centimeters long?

8. (30) Three nickels make up what percent of a dollar?

9. (39) Compare: $\frac{1}{3} \bigcirc \frac{1}{4}$

10. (9) 7208 − 6194

11. (29) \$4.32 × 50

12. (18) 5 × 5 × 7

13. (26) $4\overline{)\$31.64}$

14. (34) 8118 ÷ 9

15. (42) Use short division: $6\overline{)4500}$

16. (41) $1\frac{2}{5} + 2\frac{3}{5}$

17. (41) $\frac{8}{10} - \frac{5}{10}$

18. (41) $\frac{1}{3} - \frac{1}{3}$

19. (13, 24) \$15 − (\$3.55 + \$10 + \$0.72)

20. (21) Maria has 7 rolls of nickels. If each roll has 40 nickels in it, how many nickles does Maria have?

Name ______________________

Score ______________________

Cumulative Test 9B

Also take ***Power-Up Test 9***

Refer to this function table to answer problems **1** and **2**:

In	4	12	24
Out	1	3	6

1. (Inv. 4) What does the function do to each "in" number?

A. It subtracts 9.

B. It divides by 2.

C. It divides by 4.

D. It multiplies by 2.

2. (Inv. 4) If 8 is used as the "in" number, what will be the "out" number?

3. (44) Use an inch ruler to measure the length of this segment to the nearest eighth of an inch:

4. (43) What mixed number is half of 25?

5. (45) Which of the quadrilaterals below is not a parallelogram?

A.  **B.** 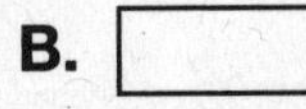

C. 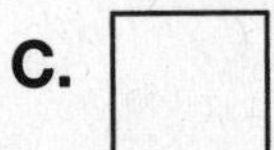 **D.** 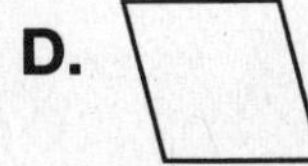

6. (40) What mixed number names the number of shaded circles shown below?

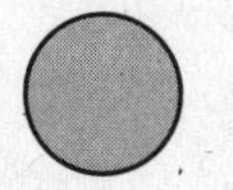 

7. (44) A key that is 50 millimeters long is how many centimeters long?

8. (30) Eight dimes make up what percent of a dollar?

9. (39) Compare: $\frac{1}{3} \bigcirc \frac{1}{2}$

10. (9) 5014 − 4362

11. (29) \$6.07 × 40

12. (18) 3 × 5 × 7

13. $6\overline{)\$75.72}$
(26)

14. $5663 \div 7$
(34)

15. Use short division: $8\overline{)1200}$
(42)

16. $3\frac{3}{5} + 1\frac{2}{5}$
(41)

17. $\frac{9}{10} - \frac{2}{10}$
(41)

18. $\frac{1}{2} - \frac{1}{2}$
(41)

19. $20 − ($6.48 + $12 + $0.95)
(13, 24)

20. Hong has 8 rolls of dimes. If each roll has 50 dimes in it, how many dimes does Hong have?
(21)

Name ______________________________

Score ______________________________

Cumulative Test 10A

Also take ***Power-Up Test 10***

1. (49) Alannah has 6 more pets than Steven. Steven has 2 more pets than Maria. Maria has 2 pets. How many pets does Alannah have?

2. (48) Write the standard form for $(8 \times 10{,}000) + (7 \times 1000) + (9 \times 1)$.

3. (47) Salome is 2 feet 5 inches tall. How many inches tall is Salome?

4. (50) There are 13 students in one line and 21 students in the other line. If the two lines were made even, how many students would be in each line?

5. (30, 37) Draw a square and shade three fourths of it. What percent of the square is shaded?

6. (44) Use a ruler to find the length of this line segment to the nearest quarter inch:

7. (44) Three meters equals how many centimeters?

8. (7) Use digits to write the number three hundred four thousand, eleven.

9. (13) $3.75 + $13.01 + $19.24

10. (13) $50 − $41.82

11. (17) 516×4

12. (29)
$$\begin{array}{r} \$3.95 \\ \times\ \ 70 \\ \hline \end{array}$$

13. (9)
$$\begin{array}{r} 3055 \\ -\ 2938 \\ \hline \end{array}$$

14. (34) $654 \div 5$

15. (26) $7\overline{)6024}$

16. (34) $\frac{954}{9}$

17. (41) $\frac{6}{7} - \frac{6}{7}$

18. (41) $7\frac{1}{5} + 3\frac{3}{5}$

19. (41) $4\frac{3}{4} - 2\frac{2}{4}$

Use the information given in this bar graph to answer the question below.

20. (Inv. 5) John made twice as many free throws as which player?

Name ______________________________

Score ______________________________

Cumulative Test 10B

Also take ***Power-Up Test 10***

1. (49) Walt is 3 years older than Ralph. Ralph is 4 years older than Henry. Walt is 48 years old. How old is Henry?

2. (48) Write the standard form for $(5 \times 1000) + (3 \times 100) + (7 \times 10)$.

3. (47) Lamar is 5 feet 10 inches tall. How many inches tall is Lamar?

4. (50) There are 12 students in one line and 20 students in the other line. If the two lines were made even, how many students would be in each line?

5. (30, 37) Draw a circle and shade three fourths of it. What percent of the circle is shaded?

6. (44) Use a ruler to find the length of this line segment to the nearest quarter inch:

7. (44) Two centimeters equals how many millimeters?

8. (7) Use digits to write the number one hundred twenty-five thousand, three hundred sixty-four.

9. (13) \$5.84 + \$12.96 + \$24

10. (13) \$100 − \$63.75

11. (17) $\begin{array}{r} 294 \\ \times \quad 3 \\ \hline \end{array}$

12. (29)
$$\begin{array}{r} \$5.08 \\ \times \quad 60 \\ \hline \end{array}$$

13. (9)
$$\begin{array}{r} 1010 \\ -\ \ 436 \\ \hline \end{array}$$

14. (34) $563 \div 4$

15. (26) $9\overline{)4000}$

16. (34) $\dfrac{864}{8}$

17. (41) $\dfrac{3}{8} - \dfrac{3}{8}$

18. (41) $3\frac{1}{3} + 2\frac{1}{3}$

19. (41) $5\frac{3}{5} - 1\frac{1}{5}$

Use the information given in this bar graph to answer the question below.

20. (Inv. 5) Bev made how many more free throws than Jason?

Name ______________________________

Score ______________________________

Cumulative Test 11A

Also take **Power-Up Test 11**

1. (50) Geraldine has four pastures with 3 horses, 5 horses, 7 horses, and 17 horses in them. If she were to switch the horses so that each pasture had the same number, how many horses would be in each pasture?

2. (46) How many is $\frac{1}{4}$ of a dozen?

3. (35) How many years were there from 1621 to 1907?

4. (33) Round 329 to the nearest ten.

5. (44, 53) The circle has a radius of 30 mm. What is the diameter of the circle in centimeters?

6. (10) Find the missing number:
$13 \times 1 = 12 + w$

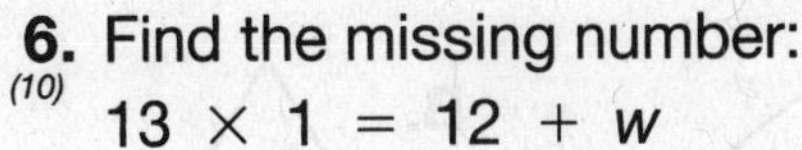

7. (53) What is the perimeter of this rectangle?

6 in.

3 in.

8. (Inv. 4) At the library, 48 people returned books on Monday. Then 40 people returned books on Tuesday. On Wednesday, 32 people returned books. If this pattern continues, how many people will return books on Friday?

9. (48) Write the standard form for $(4 \times 100{,}000) + (8 \times 10{,}000) + (6 \times 10) + (5 \times 1)$.

10. (36) Which triangle appears to be equilateral?

A. 

B.

C.

D.

11. (6) $3164 + 721 + 145$

12. (9) $5280 - 4933$

13. (29)

$$\begin{array}{r} \$2.75 \\ \times \quad 30 \\ \hline \end{array}$$

14. (51)

$$\begin{array}{r} 52 \\ \times \ 45 \\ \hline \end{array}$$

15. (34) $\frac{3608}{4}$

16. (54) $20\overline{)680}$

17. (43) $3 + \frac{1}{3}$

18. (43) $5\frac{2}{3} - 3$

19. (30, 37) Draw a square. Shade all but $\frac{1}{4}$ of it. What percent of the square is shaded?

20. (52) Use words to name 32180795.

Name ______________________________

Score ______________________________

Also take ***Power-Up Test 11***

1. Coach Clausing has four teams of golfers with 5 players, 7 players, 8 players, and 8 players. If he were to switch the players so that each team had the same number, how many players would be on each team?
(50)

2. How many is $\frac{2}{3}$ of a dozen?
(46)

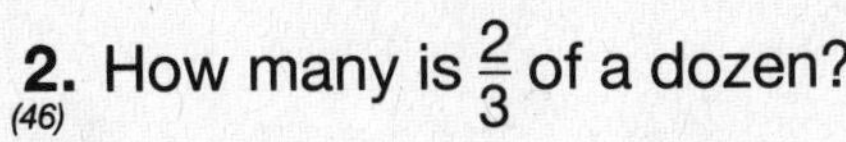

3. How many years were there from 1492 to 1601?
(35)

4. Round 679 to the nearest ten.
(33)

5. The circle has a radius of 40 mm. What is the diameter of the circle in centimeters?
(44, 53)

6. Find the missing number:
(10)
$12 \times 1 = 12 + w$

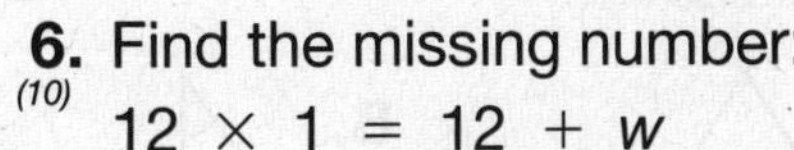

7. What is the perimeter of this rectangle?
(53)

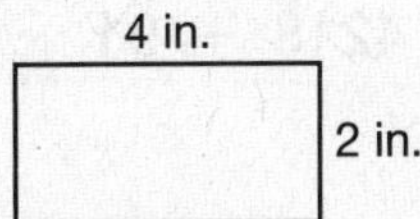

8. At the library, 56 people borrowed books on Monday. Then 48 people borrowed books on Tuesday. On Wednesday, 40 people borrowed books. If this pattern continues, how many people will borrow books on Friday?
(Inv. 4)

9. Write the standard form for $(3 \times 100{,}000) + (8 \times 1000) + (4 \times 100) + (3 \times 1)$.
(48)

10. (36) Which triangle appears to be equilateral?

A. △ **B.** ◺

C. ◿ **D.** △

11. (6) 3625 + 4218 + 91

12. (9) 3426 − 2643

13. (29) $$\begin{array}{r} \$1.25 \\ \times \quad 40 \\ \hline \end{array}$$

14. (51) $$\begin{array}{r} 46 \\ \times \; 35 \\ \hline \end{array}$$

15. (34) $\frac{3272}{8}$

16. (54) $20\overline{)640}$

17. (43) $\frac{3}{4} + 2$

18. (43) $6\frac{1}{2} - 4$

19. (30, 37) Draw a circle. Shade all but $\frac{1}{4}$ of it. What percent of the circle is shaded?

20. (52) Use words to name 27849531.

Name ______________________

Score ______________________

Also take **Power-Up Test 12**

1. (57) The spinner below is divided into five equal-sized sectors. What is the probability that the spinner will stop on a number greater than 3?

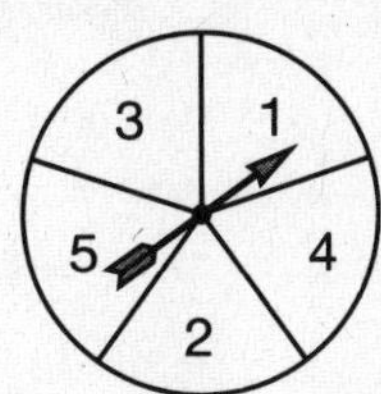

2. (20) The dividend is 125. The divisor is 5. What is the quotient?

3. (52) Use digits to write the number ninety-six million, eleven thousand, two hundred forty-one.

4. (52) Which digit is in the hundred-thousands place in 36,792,045?

5. (50) In four compartments there are 12 bundles, 2 bundles, 7 bundles, and 11 bundles. If the bundles were rearranged so that each compartment held the same number of bundles, how many bundles would be in each compartment?

6. (53) What is the perimeter of this triangle?

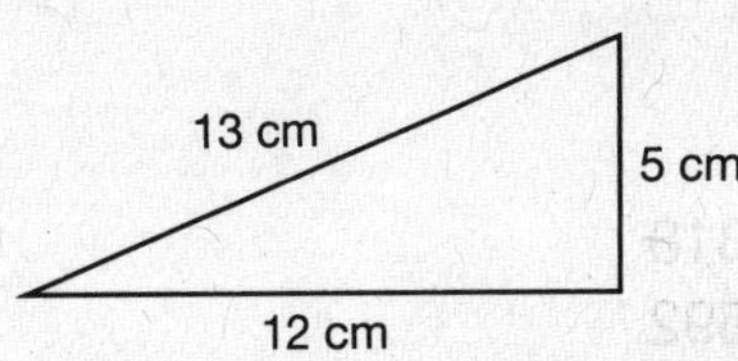

7. (53) The radius of this circle is 8 cm. What is its diameter?

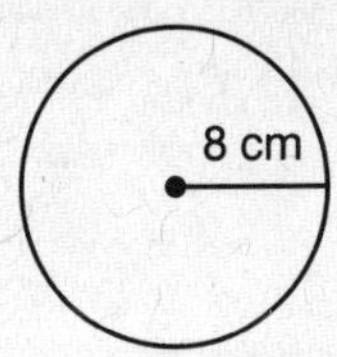

8. (60) Three fifths of the students are boys. What fraction of the students are girls?

9. (57) The weather forecast states that the chance of rain is 80%. This means that rain is

A. impossible **B.** unlikely

C. likely **D.** certain

10. (46) Vijay has finished $\frac{1}{5}$ of the 20 questions. How many questions has he finished?

11. (6)
$$\begin{array}{r} 2318 \\ 592 \\ +\ 624 \\ \hline \end{array}$$

12. (9)
$$\begin{array}{r} 4651 \\ -\ 3748 \\ \hline \end{array}$$

13. (55)
$$\begin{array}{r} 525 \\ \times\ 144 \\ \hline \end{array}$$

14. (56)
$$\begin{array}{r} 691 \\ \times\ 370 \\ \hline \end{array}$$

15. (54) $725 \div 10$

16. (58) Divide and write the quotient as a mixed number: $7\overline{)8284}$

17. (54) $30\overline{)\$9.30}$

18. (59) $7\frac{1}{5} + 2\frac{4}{5}$

19. (59) $1 - \frac{1}{7}$

20. (13, 24) $\$30 - (\$19.75 + \$3 + \$0.83)$

Name ______________________________

Score ______________________________

Cumulative Test 12B

Also take **Power-Up Test 12**

1. (57) The spinner below is divided into five equal-sized sectors. What is the probability that the spinner will stop on a number less than three?

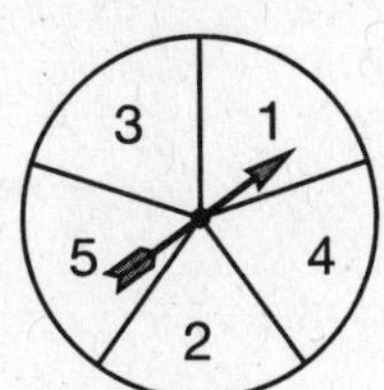

2. (20) The divisor is 8. The dividend is 760. What is the quotient?

3. (52) Use digits to write the number twenty-three million, five hundred thirty-two thousand, six hundred twelve.

4. (52) Which digit is in the millions place in 19,375,468?

5. (50) In three stacks there are 15 books, 9 books, and 9 books. If the books were rearranged so that each stack had the same number of books, how many books would be in each stack?

6. (53) What is the perimeter of this triangle?

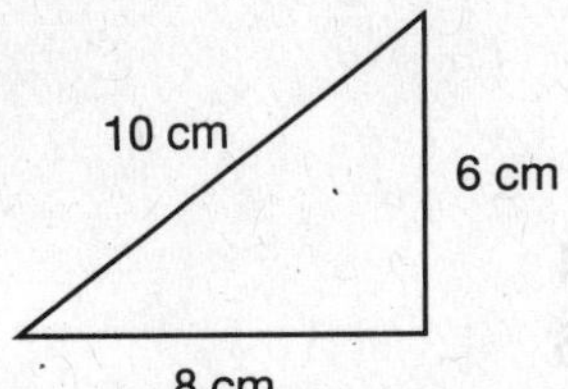

7. (53) The radius of this circle is 5 cm. What is its diameter?

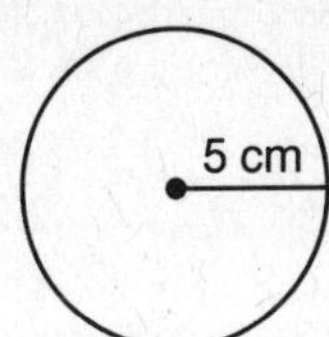

8. (60) Two fifths of the students are boys. What fraction of the students are girls?

9. (57) The weather forecast states that the chance of rain is 20%. This means that rain is

A. impossible **B.** unlikely

C. likely **D.** certain

10. (46) Jenny has finished $\frac{1}{10}$ of the 20 questions. How many questions has she finished?

11. (6)

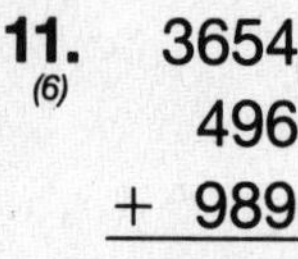

$$\begin{array}{r} 3654 \\ 496 \\ +\ 989 \\ \hline \end{array}$$

12. (9)

$$\begin{array}{r} 3105 \\ -\ 1530 \\ \hline \end{array}$$

13. (55)

$$\begin{array}{r} 325 \\ \times\ 412 \\ \hline \end{array}$$

14. (56)

$$\begin{array}{r} 304 \\ \times\ 230 \\ \hline \end{array}$$

15. (54) $365 \div 10$

16. (58) Divide and write the quotient as a mixed number: $6\overline{)6043}$

17. (54)

$20\overline{)\$3.20}$

18. (59) $6\frac{2}{3} + 2\frac{1}{3}$

19. (59) $1 - \frac{2}{5}$

20. (13, 24) \$20 − (\$8 + \$6.34 + \$0.64)

Name ______________________________

Score ______________________________

Cumulative Test 13A

Also take **Power-Up Test 13**

1. (50) In one room there are 55 chairs. In the other room there are 25 chairs. If some chairs are moved so that the rooms have the same number of chairs, then how many chairs will be in each room?

2. (60) Nadia has eaten $\frac{1}{5}$ of her cereal. What fraction of her cereal is left to eat?

3. (35) From 1895 to 1985 was how many decades?

4. (62) Estimate the product of 64 and 22 by rounding both numbers to the nearest ten before multiplying.

5. (33) Round 3286 to the nearest hundred.

6. (31, 61) Which angle appears to be an obtuse angle?

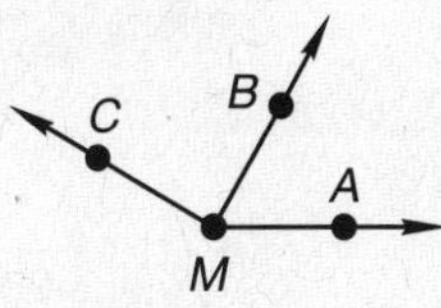

A. ∠*AMB* **B.** ∠*AMC* **C.** ∠*BMC*

7. (38) On this number line, the arrow is pointing to what mixed number?

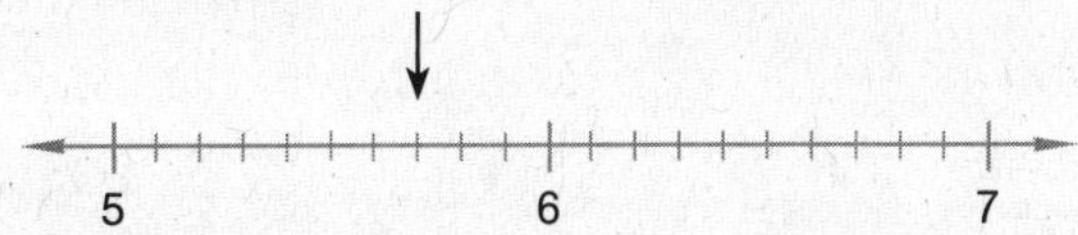

8. (57) If a number cube is rolled once, what is the probability of rolling a four?

9. (53) **a.** What is the length of this rectangle?

b. What is the perimeter of this rectangle?

4 cm

3 cm

10. $4p = 32$
(18)

11. $\frac{4}{7} + \frac{3}{7}$
(41)

12. $7 - 5\frac{2}{3}$
(63)

13. $2 - \frac{1}{3}$
(63)

14. $6468 - 979$
(9)

15. $\$12 - (\$7 + \$4.78)$
(13, 24)

16. $\begin{array}{r} 483 \\ \times\ 275 \\ \hline \end{array}$
(55)

17. $9041 \div 6$
(34)

18. $40\overline{)840}$
(54)

19. What is the place value of the 5 in \$3.75?
(64)

20. Divide and write the quotient as a mixed number: $\frac{27}{4}$
(58)

Name ______________________________

Score ______________________________

Cumulative Test 13B

Also take ***Power-Up Test 13***

1. (50) In one line there are 21 students. In the other line there are 11 students. If some students move from the longer line to the shorter line so that the lines are even, then how many students will be in each line?

2. (60) Kent has read $\frac{1}{3}$ of his book. What fraction of his book is left to read?

3. (35) From 1776 to 1826 was how many decades?

4. (62) Estimate the product of 73 and 37 by rounding both numbers to the nearest ten before multiplying.

5. (33) Round 1679 to the nearest hundred.

6. (31, 61) Which angle appears to be a right angle?

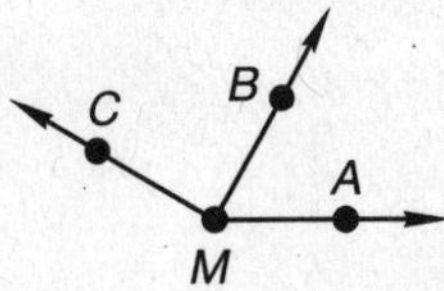

A. ∠*AMB** **B.** ∠*AMC* **C.** ∠*BMC*

7. (38) On this number line, the arrow is pointing to what mixed number?

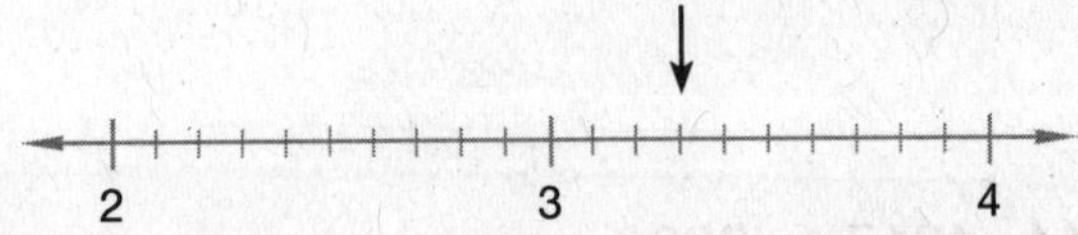

8. (57) If a number cube is rolled once, what is the probability of rolling a two?

9. (53) **a.** What is the length of this rectangle?

b. What is the perimeter of this rectangle?

2 cm

1 cm

10. $8n = 72$
(18)

11. $\frac{1}{3} + \frac{2}{3}$
(41)

12. $6 - 3\frac{1}{3}$
(63)

13. $3 - \frac{1}{4}$
(63)

14. $4217 - 363$
(9)

15. $10 − ($4 + $3.75)
(13, 24)

16. 132×325
(55)

17. $4354 \div 5$
(34)

18. $30\overline{)480}$
(54)

19. What is the place value of the 3 in $17.34?
(64)

20. Divide and write the quotient as a mixed number: $\frac{23}{5}$
(58)

Name ____________________

Score ____________________

Cumulative Test 14A

Also take ***Power-Up Test 14***

1. (49) Paolo bought three juices for $0.77 each. If he gave the clerk $5.00, how much money should he get back?

2. (25) List the factors of 24 that are also factors of 32.

3. (67) Name the shaded part of this square

a. as a fraction.

b. as a decimal number.

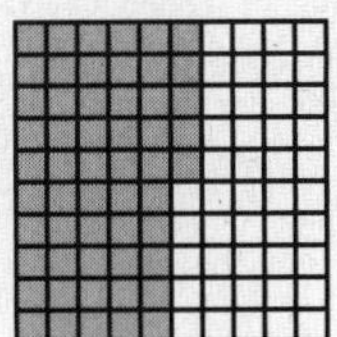

4. (68) Use words to write the decimal number 290.37.

5. (67) Write the fraction $\frac{19}{100}$ as a decimal number.

6. (68) Use digits to write the decimal number eight and seven tenths.

7. (64) Which digit in 457.89 is in the tenths place?

8. (66) Find the length of the line segment below to the nearest tenth of a centimeter:

9. (69) Compare: 0.3 ◯ 0.03

10. (62) Estimate the product of 41 and 76.

11. (6) 471 + 18 + 924 + 3240 + 1

12. (9)

$$\begin{array}{r} 13{,}500 \\ -\ 12{,}876 \\ \hline \end{array}$$

13. (56)

$$\begin{array}{r} 924 \\ \times\ 350 \\ \hline \end{array}$$

14. (34) $\dfrac{4214}{7}$

15. (18, 29) $35 \times 60 \times 2$

16. (34) $7\overline{)980}$

17. (54) $\$98.40 \div 60$

18. (24, 63) $7 - \left(4\frac{2}{5} - 1\frac{1}{5}\right)$

19. (59) $1\frac{2}{5} + 3\frac{2}{5} + 5\frac{1}{5}$

20. (58) Divide and write the quotient as a mixed number: $\dfrac{19}{3}$

Name ______________________________

Score ______________________________

Cumulative Test 14B

Also take **Power-Up Test 14**

1. (49) Avi bought two batteries for $0.89 each. If he gave the clerk $5.00, how much money should he get back?

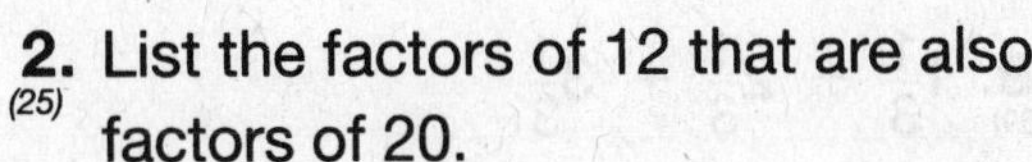

2. (25) List the factors of 12 that are also factors of 20.

3. (67) Name the shaded part of this square

a. as a fraction.

b. as a decimal number.

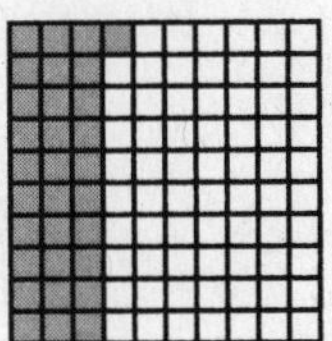

4. (68) Use words to write the decimal number 78.46.

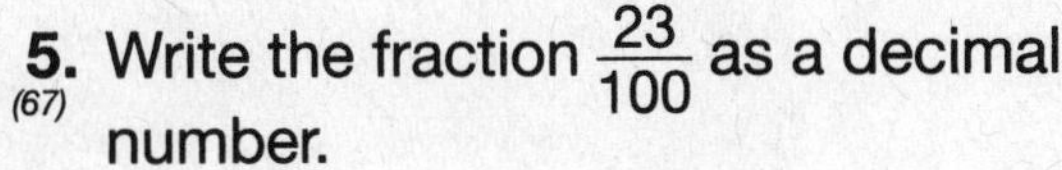

5. (67) Write the fraction $\frac{23}{100}$ as a decimal number.

6. (68) Use digits to write the decimal number twelve and one tenth.

7. (64) Which digit in 136.27 is in the hundredths place?

8. (66) Find the length of the line segment below to the nearest tenth of a centimeter:

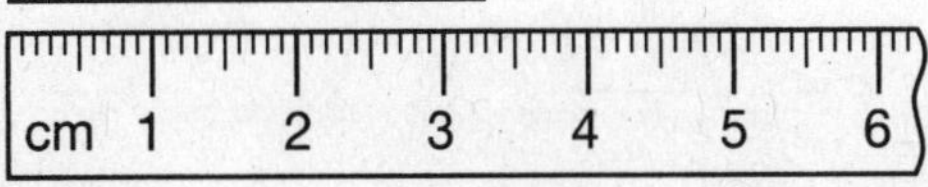

9. (69) Compare: 0.5 ◯ 0.05

10. (62) Estimate the product of 32 and 59.

11. (6) 363 + 45 + 2715 + 8 + 17

12. (9)
$$\begin{array}{r} 20{,}000 \\ -\ 14{,}258 \\ \hline \end{array}$$

13. (56)
$$\begin{array}{r} 136 \\ \times\ 250 \\ \hline \end{array}$$

14. (34) $\dfrac{5663}{7}$

15. (18, 29) $25 \times 30 \times 4$

16. (34) $6\overline{)960}$

17. (54) $\$65.40 \div 30$

18. (24, 63) $6 - \left(4\frac{1}{3} - 2\right)$

19. (59) $1\frac{1}{3} + 2\frac{1}{3} + 3\frac{1}{3}$

20. (58) Divide and write the quotient as a mixed number: $\dfrac{16}{5}$

Name ______________________________

Score ______________________________

Cumulative Test 15A

Also take ***Power-Up Test 15***

1. (23, 59) Arrange these fractions in order from least to greatest:

$$\frac{5}{8}, \frac{7}{7}, \frac{1}{3}, \frac{2}{4}$$

2. (75) Write the fraction $\frac{11}{4}$ as a mixed number.

3. (74) Three feet equals one yard. One mile equals 1760 yards. Two miles equals how many feet?

4. (68) Use digits to write the decimal number eight and four hundredths.

5. (64) Which digit in 123.45 is in the tenths place?

6. (73)

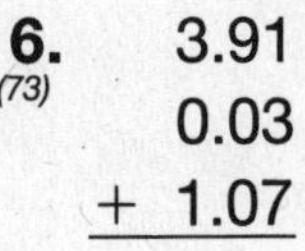

$$\begin{array}{r} 3.91 \\ 0.03 \\ +\ 1.07 \\ \hline \end{array}$$

7. (71) Name the shaded part of this square

a. as a fraction

b. as a decimal number

c. as a percent

8. (33) Round 3721 to the nearest hundred.

9. (70) Compare: 2.5 ◯ 2.500

10. (58) Divide 891 by 40 and write the quotient as a mixed number.

11. (70) \$2.54 + 93¢ + \$0.72

12. $\$2.28 - 79¢$
(70)

13. $\begin{array}{r} 3.208 \\ -\ 2.6 \\ \hline \end{array}$
(73)

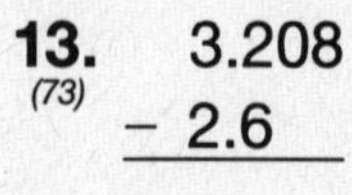

14. $\begin{array}{r} \$0.93 \\ \times\ \ \ \ \ 7 \\ \hline \end{array}$
(17)

15. $8 - \left(4\frac{8}{11} - 2\frac{6}{11}\right)$
(24, 63)

16. $4\frac{2}{5} + 3\frac{3}{5}$
(59)

17. The length of $\overline{MN}$ is 30 mm. Segment *NO* is 30 mm long. Find the length of $\overline{MO}$ in **centimeters.**
(61, 74)

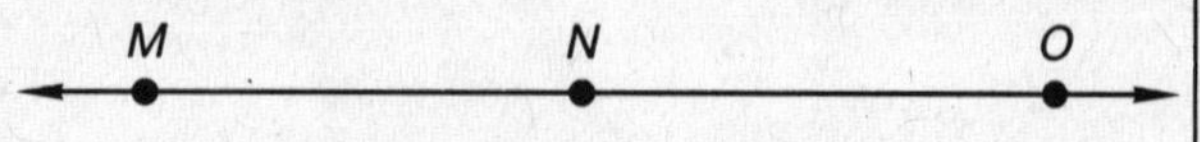

18. Draw a parallelogram that is not a rectangle.
(45)

A rectangular room is 6 yards long and 4 yards wide. Use this information to answer problems **19** and **20**.

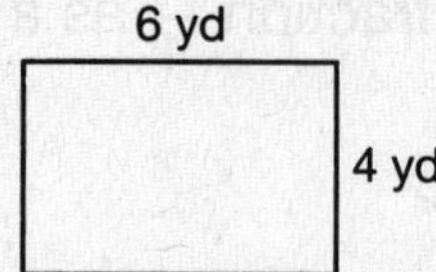

19. What is the perimeter of the room?
(53)

20. What is the area of the room?
(72)

Name ______________________________

Score ______________________________

Cumulative Test 15B

Also take ***Power-Up Test 15***

1. (23, 59) Arrange these fractions in order from least to greatest:

$$\frac{1}{3}, \frac{3}{6}, \frac{5}{5}, \frac{3}{4}$$

2. (75) Write the fraction $\frac{9}{5}$ as a mixed number.

3. (74) Twelve inches equals one foot. Three feet equals one yard. Three yards equals how many inches?

4. (68) Use digits to write the decimal number twelve and twenty-one hundredths.

5. (64) Which digit in 123.45 is in the hundredths place?

6. (73)

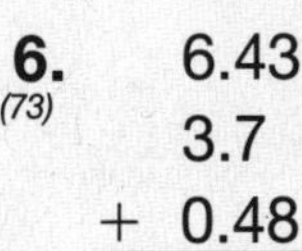

$$\begin{array}{r} 6.43 \\ 3.7 \\ +\ 0.48 \\ \hline \end{array}$$

7. (71) Name the shaded part of this square

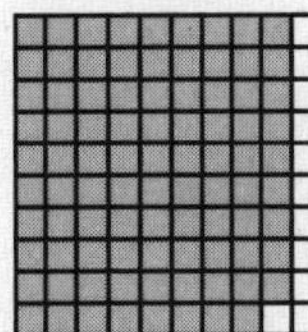

a. as a fraction

b. as a decimal number

c. as a percent

8. (33) Round 2624 to the nearest hundred.

9. (70) Compare: 1.2 ◯ 1.20

10. (58) Divide 931 by 30 and write the quotient as a mixed number.

11. (70) \$3.67 + 58¢ + \$4

12. $1.14 − 68¢
(70)

13. $\begin{array}{r} 5.367 \\ -\ 1.4 \\ \hline \end{array}$
(73)

14. $\begin{array}{r} \$0.45 \\ \times\quad 6 \\ \hline \end{array}$
(17)

15. $5 - \left(2\frac{2}{3} - \frac{1}{3}\right)$
(24, 63)

16. $3\frac{2}{3} + 1\frac{1}{3}$
(59)

17. The length of $\overline{MN}$ is 40 mm. Segment *NO* is 10 mm long. Find the length of $\overline{MO}$ in **centimeters.**
(61, 74)

18. Draw a parallelogram that has right angles.
(45)

A rectangular room is 5 yards long and 4 yards wide. Use this information to answer problems **19** and **20.**

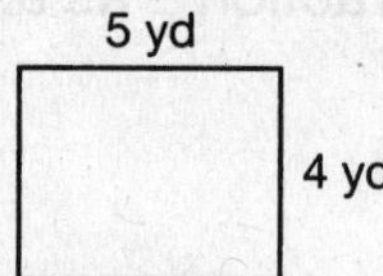

19. What is the perimeter of the room?
(53)

20. What is the area of the room?
(72)

Name ______________________________

Score ______________________________

Cumulative Test 16A

Also take ***Power-Up Test 16***

1. (49) Akemi bought three novels for $3.95 each and a bookmark for 35¢. What was the total cost of the items?

2. (78) Write 2^5 as a whole number.

3. (67) Write $\frac{83}{100}$ as a decimal number.

4. (74) How many millimeters are in 62.5 meters?

5. (77) One kilogram equals 1000 grams. Five kilograms of sugar is how many grams of sugar?

6. (64) Which digit in 4.803 is in the same place as the 7 in 608.72?

7. (79) Compare: $\frac{2}{3}$ ◯ $\frac{2}{3} \times \frac{3}{3}$

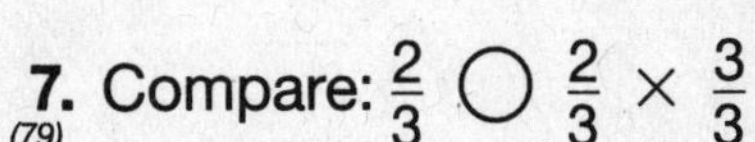

8. (79) Write a fraction equal to $\frac{2}{3}$ that has a denominator of 24.

9. (80) Name all the prime numbers between 20 and 30.

10. (66) Find the length of this segment to the nearest tenth of a centimeter:

cm 1 2 3 4

11. (70) $4 + $3.26 + 19¢ + $28 + 7¢

12. (73)

$$\begin{array}{r} 19.05 \\ 3.26 \\ +\ 4.7 \\ \hline \end{array}$$

13. (73)

$$\begin{array}{r} 41.35 \\ -\ 18.6 \\ \hline \end{array}$$

14. (54) $\frac{6690}{30}$

15. (17) $\$2.41 \times 8$

16. (18, 29) $20 \times 70 \times 50$

17. (26) $3\overline{)\$13.23}$

18. (75) $\frac{3}{6} + \frac{4}{6}$

19. (76) 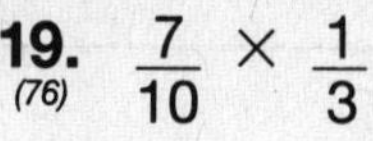
$\frac{7}{10} \times \frac{1}{3}$

20. (61) 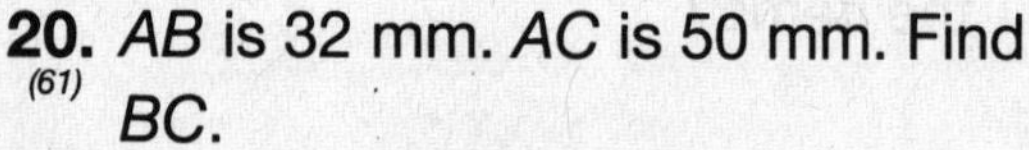
AB is 32 mm. *AC* is 50 mm. Find *BC*.

Name ______________________________

Score ______________________________

Cumulative Test 16B

Also take ***Power-Up Test 16***

1. (49) Jonathan bought two models for \$2.75 each and a tube of glue for 95¢. What was the total cost of the items?

2. (78) Write 3^3 as a whole number.

3. (67) Write $\frac{3}{100}$ as a decimal number.

4. (74) How many centimeters are in 8.5 kilometers?

5. (77) One pound equals 16 ounces. Three pounds of grapes weighs how many ounces?

6. (64) Which digit in 36.4 is in the same place as the 7 in 127.53?

7. (79) Compare: $\frac{1}{2} \bigcirc \frac{1}{2} \times \frac{2}{2}$

8. (79) Write a fraction equal to $\frac{3}{4}$ that has a denominator of 12.

9. (80) The first three prime numbers are 2, 3, and 5. What are the next three prime numbers?

10. (66) Find the length of this segment to the nearest tenth of a centimeter:

cm 1 2 3 4

11. (70) \$8 + \$1.45 + 76¢ + \$12 + 5¢

12. (73)

$$\begin{array}{r} 13.64 \\ 2.4 \\ +\ 15.7 \\ \hline \end{array}$$

13. (73)

$$\begin{array}{r} 36.45 \\ -\ 9.6 \\ \hline \end{array}$$

14. (54) $\frac{4320}{20}$

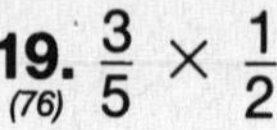

15. (17) $\begin{array}{r} \$3.45 \\ \times \quad 5 \\ \hline \end{array}$

16. (18, 29) $30 \times 40 \times 50$

17. (26) $8\overline{)\$46.00}$

18. (75) $\frac{3}{5} + \frac{4}{5}$

19. (76) $\frac{3}{5} \times \frac{1}{2}$

20. (61) *AB* is 25 mm. *AC* is 45 mm. Find *BC*.

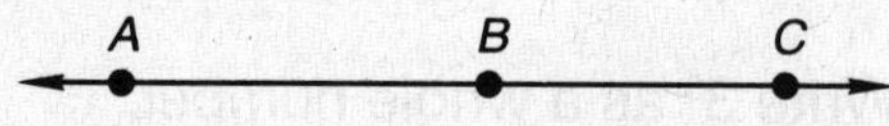

Name ____________________

Score ____________________

Cumulative Test 17A

Also take ***Power-Up Test 17***

1. Each of these numbers divides 620 without a remainder except
(22, 42)

A. 10 **B.** 5 **C.** 3 **D.** 2

Refer to quadrilateral *ABCD* to answer problems **2** and **3**.

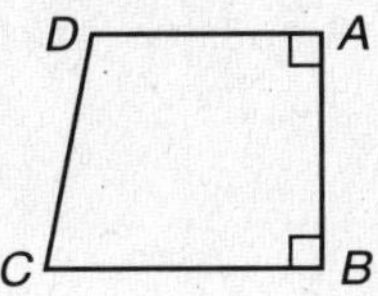

2. Angle *DCB* is acute. Which angle is obtuse?
(31, 61)

3. Which segment is perpendicular to $\overline{AD}$?
(31, 61)

4. What is the name of this shape?
(83)

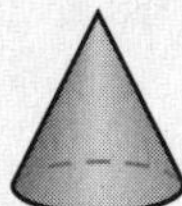

A. cone **B.** cylinder

C. cube **D.** pyramid

5. a. What number is $\frac{2}{3}$ of 21?
(46)

b. What number is $\frac{1}{3}$ of 21?

6. One sixth of the 30 students were absent. How many students were absent?
(46)

7. a. Find the greatest common factor (GCF) of 24 and 32.
(82)

b. Use the GCF of 24 and 32 to reduce $\frac{24}{32}$.

8. How many quarts are in two gallons?
(85)

9. Reduce each fraction:
(81)

a. $\frac{14}{21}$ **b.** $\frac{9}{15}$ **c.** $\frac{7}{14}$

10.
(73)

$$\begin{array}{r} 13.21 \\ 4.049 \\ +\ 132.2 \\ \hline \end{array}$$

11. (73)
$$\begin{array}{r} 19.502 \\ -\ \ 8.807 \\ \hline \end{array}$$

12. (78) 4^3

13. (78) $7\overline{)\$22.12}$

14. (9)
$$\begin{array}{r} 3040 \\ -\ 2876 \\ \hline \end{array}$$

15. (56)
$$\begin{array}{r} 790 \\ \times\ 206 \\ \hline \end{array}$$

16. (54) $\dfrac{2040}{60}$

17. (75) 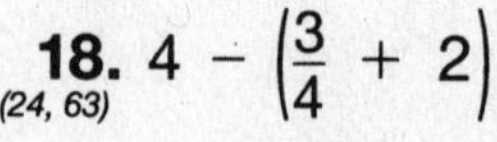
$6\frac{4}{5} + 3\frac{3}{5}$

18. (24, 63) $4 - \left(\frac{3}{4} + 2\right)$

19. (79) Compare: $\frac{1}{2} \times \frac{4}{4} \bigcirc \frac{1}{2} \times \frac{3}{3}$

20. (66, 72) What is the area of this square?

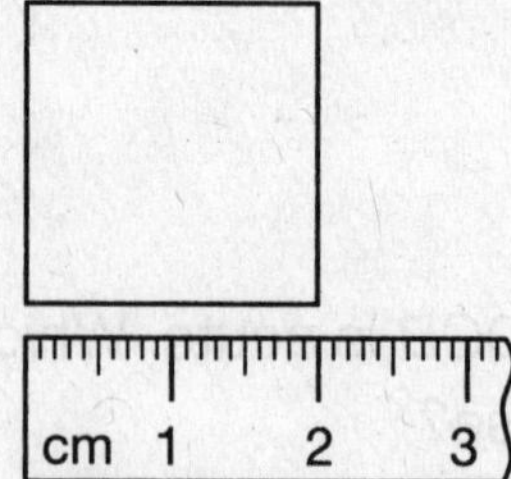

Name ______________________________

Score ______________________________

Cumulative Test 17B

Also take **Power-Up Test 17**

1. Each of the following numbers divides 320 without a remainder except
(22, 42)

A. 2 **B.** 3 **C.** 5 **D.** 10

Refer to quadrilateral *ABCD* to answer problems **2** and **3.**

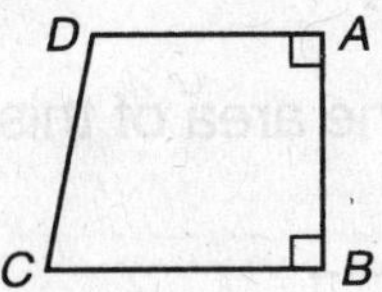

2. Angle *ADC* is obtuse. Which angle is acute?
(31, 61)

3. Which segment is parallel to $\overline{AD}$?
(31, 61)

4. What is the name of this shape?
(83)

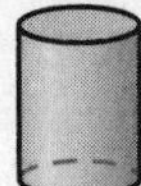

A. cone **B.** cylinder

C. cube **D.** pyramid

5. a. What number is $\frac{1}{4}$ of 20?
(46)

b. What number is $\frac{3}{4}$ of 20?

6. One fifth of the 30 students were absent. How many students were absent?
(46)

7. a. Find the greatest common factor (GCF) of 14 and 21.
(82)

b. Use the GCF of 14 and 21 to reduce $\frac{14}{21}$.

8. How many milliliters are in three liters?
(85)

9. Reduce each fraction:
(81)

a. $\frac{9}{12}$ **b.** $\frac{4}{8}$ **c.** $\frac{18}{27}$

10.
(73)

$$\begin{array}{r} 56.43 \\ 7.923 \\ +\ 145.8 \\ \hline \end{array}$$

11. (73)
$$\begin{array}{r} 23.567 \\ -\ 14.63 \\ \hline \end{array}$$

12. (78) 5^3

13. (26) $8\overline{)\$26.00}$

14. (9)
$$\begin{array}{r} 6010 \\ -\ 5984 \\ \hline \end{array}$$

15. (56)
$$\begin{array}{r} 560 \\ \times\ 704 \\ \hline \end{array}$$

16. (54) $\frac{3760}{40}$

17. (75) $3\frac{2}{3} + 3\frac{2}{3}$

18. (24, 63) $4 - \left(\frac{2}{3} + 1\right)$

19. (79) Compare: $\frac{2}{3} \times \frac{2}{2} \bigcirc \frac{2}{3} \times \frac{3}{3}$

20. (66, 72) What is the area of this square?

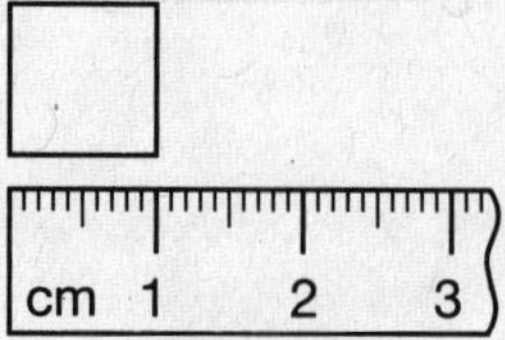

Name ______________________________

Score ______________________________

Cumulative Test 18A

Also take ***Power-Up Test 18***

1. Class starts at 8:30 a.m. It takes Russ 25 minutes to bicycle to school. At what time should he start for class if he wants to get there 15 minutes early?
(28, 49)

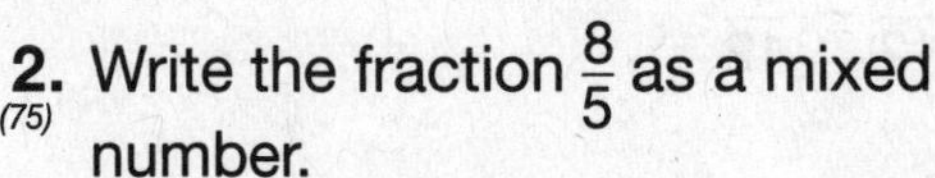

2. Write the fraction $\frac{8}{5}$ as a mixed number.
(75)

3. Reduce: $\frac{36}{48}$
(90)

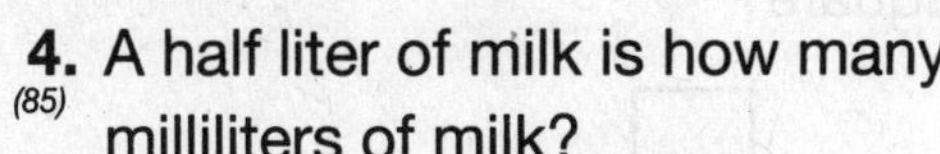

4. A half liter of milk is how many milliliters of milk?
(85)

5. A volleyball has the shape of a
(83)

A. cylinder **B.** sphere

C. pyramid **D.** rectangular solid

Refer to quadrilateral *ABCD* to answer problems **6** and **7**.

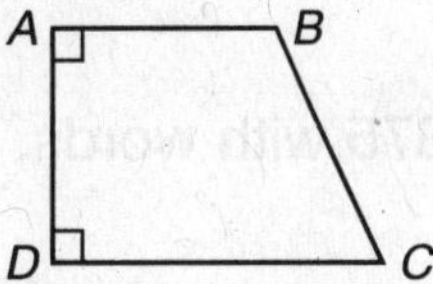

6. Which segment is parallel to $\overline{AB}$?
(31, 61)

7. Which angle is an obtuse angle?
(31, 61)

8. What number is $\frac{2}{3}$ of 21?
(86)

9. What is the median of these seven scores?
(84)

90, 75, 75, 85, 80, 90, 75

10. (79) Write a fraction equal to $\frac{3}{4}$ that has a denominator of 8.

11. (68) Write 0.375 with words.

12. (9) 24,896 − 8934

13. (56) 718 × 170

14. (26) $9\overline{)\$53.01}$

15. (76) $\frac{3}{4} \times \frac{1}{2}$

16. (78) $\sqrt{36}$

17. (87) $\frac{2}{3} \div \frac{2}{3}$

18. (90) $\frac{11}{12} - \frac{7}{12}$

19. (90) $1\frac{5}{9} + 3\frac{1}{9}$

20. (53, 66) What is the perimeter of this square?

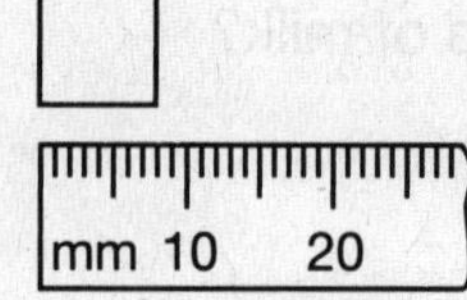

Name ______________________

Score ______________________

Cumulative Test 18B

Also take **Power-Up Test 18**

1. (28, 49) School starts at 8:15 a.m. It takes Heather 15 minutes to walk to school. At what time should she start for school if she wants to get there 10 minutes early?

2. (75) Write the fraction $\frac{7}{3}$ as a mixed number.

3. (90) Reduce: $\frac{16}{24}$

4. (85) A half gallon of milk is how many quarts of milk?

5. (83) A brick has the shape of a

A. cylinder **B.** sphere

C. pyramid **D.** rectangular solid

Refer to quadrilateral *ABCD* to answer problems **6** and **7**.

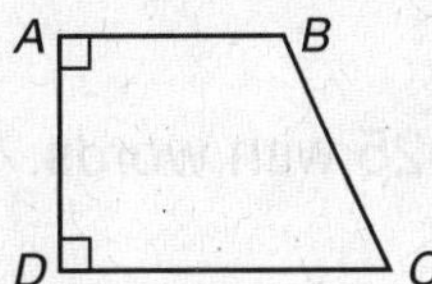

6. (31, 61) Which segment is perpendicular to $\overline{AB}$?

7. (31, 61) Which angle is an acute angle?

8. (86) What number is $\frac{3}{8}$ of 24?

9. (84) What is the median of these seven scores?

90, 80, 100, 80, 85, 90, 80

10. Write a fraction equal to $\frac{2}{3}$ that has a denominator of 6.
(79)

11. Write 0.125 with words.
(68)

12. $36,015 - 3156$
(9)

13. 506×240
(56)

14. $8\overline{)\$12.64}$
(26)

15. $\frac{3}{8} \times \frac{1}{2}$
(76)

16. $\sqrt{16}$
(78)

17. $\frac{3}{4} \div \frac{3}{4}$
(87)

18. $\frac{5}{6} - \frac{1}{6}$
(90)

19. $3\frac{1}{8} + 1\frac{5}{8}$
(90)

20. What is the perimeter of this square?
(53, 66)

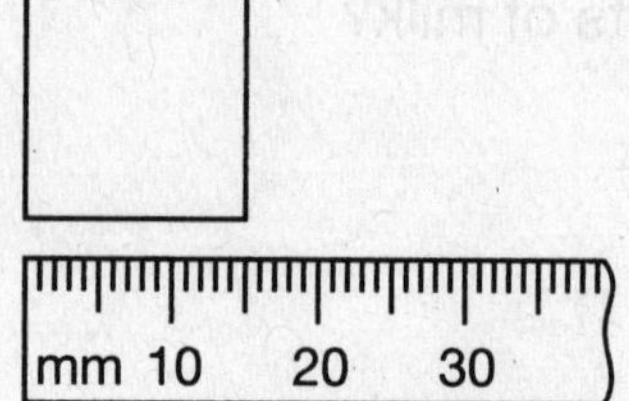

Name ______________________________

Score ______________________________

Cumulative Test 19A

Also take **Power-Up Test 19**

1. What is the reciprocal of $\frac{4}{5}$?
(95)

2. Write fractions equal to $\frac{1}{7}$ and $\frac{1}{2}$ with denominators of 14. Then add the fractions.
(79)

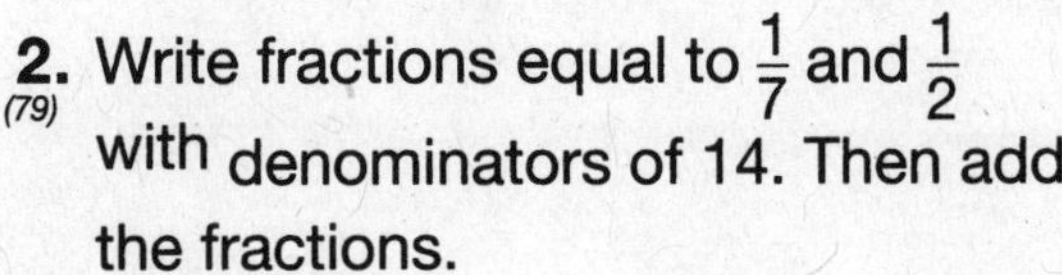

3. Diego had 2 dozen model cars which he kept in 3 cases. How many cars were in each case?
(21)

4. a. What number is $\frac{1}{5}$ of 80?
(86)

b. What number is $\frac{2}{5}$ of 80?

5. Name the shaded part of this rectangle
(71)

a. as a reduced fraction.
b. as a decimal number.
c. as a percent.

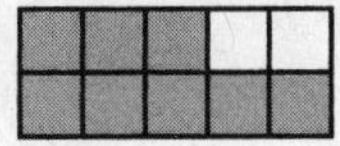

6. List the numbers below in order from least to greatest.
(69)

1, 0.2, $\frac{2}{3}$

7. Write the length of this segment
(66)

a. in centimeters.

b. in millimeters.

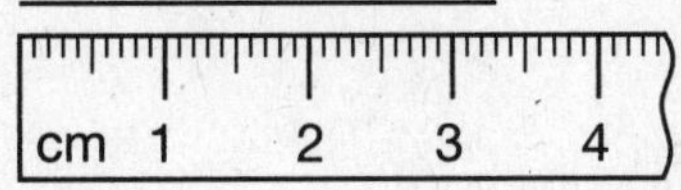

8. Reduce: $\frac{24}{16}$
(91)

9. $\frac{4}{7} = \frac{r}{21}$
(79)

10.
(73)

$$\begin{array}{r} 32.14 \\ 3.89 \\ +\ 10.2 \\ \hline \end{array}$$

11. (9)
$$\begin{array}{r} 5083 \\ -\ 4235 \\ \hline \end{array}$$

12. (51)
$$\begin{array}{r} \$13.21 \\ \times\quad 27 \\ \hline \end{array}$$

13. (54) $20\overline{)\$26.00}$

14. (78) $\sqrt{64}$

15. (94) $23\overline{)1173}$

16. (90) $4\frac{5}{8} - 2\frac{3}{8}$

17. (91) $2\frac{2}{3} + 3\frac{2}{3}$

18. (86) $\frac{5}{6} \times 5$

19. (70) $8.23 + 21¢ + $4

20. (70) 16 × 25¢

Name ______________________________

Score ______________________________

Cumulative Test 19B

Also take **Power-Up Test 19**

1. (95) What is the reciprocal of $\frac{3}{2}$?

2. (79) Write fractions equal to $\frac{1}{3}$ and $\frac{1}{4}$ with denominators of 12. Then add the fractions.

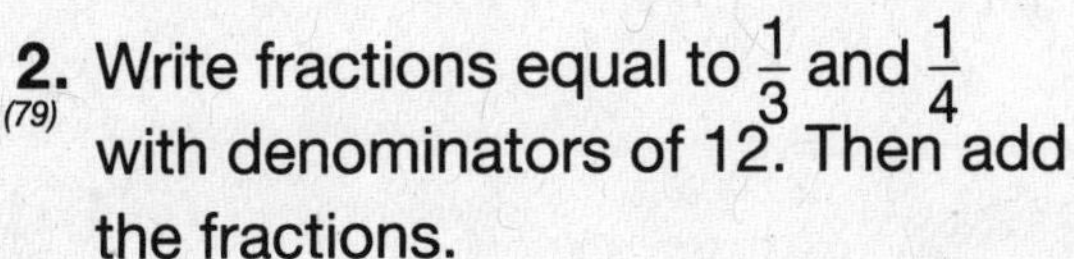

3. (21) Sally had 3 dozen fig trees which she planted in 4 rows. How many trees were in each row?

4. (86) **a.** What number is $\frac{1}{3}$ of 60?

b. What number is $\frac{2}{3}$ of 60?

5. (71) Name the shaded part of this rectangle

a. as a reduced fraction.

b. as a decimal number.

c. as a percent.

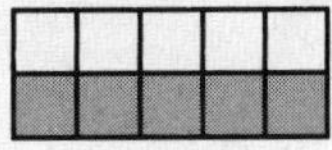

6. (69) List the numbers below in order from least to greatest.

$\frac{1}{2}$, 0.1, 0

7. (66) Write the length of this segment

a. in centimeters.

b. in millimeters.

cm 1 2 3 4

8. (91) Reduce: $\frac{20}{12}$

9. (79) $\frac{3}{5} = \frac{n}{10}$

10. (73)

$$\begin{array}{r} 43.1 \\ 8.52 \\ +\ 16.8 \\ \hline \end{array}$$

11. (9)
$$\begin{array}{r} 3105 \\ -\ 2948 \\ \hline \end{array}$$

12. (51)
$$\begin{array}{r} \$4.75 \\ \times\ \ \ 36 \\ \hline \end{array}$$

13. (54) $10\overline{)\$12.00}$

14. (78) $\sqrt{49}$

15. (94) $19\overline{)798}$

16. (90) $5\frac{5}{6} - 1\frac{1}{6}$

17. (91) $3\frac{3}{4} + 1\frac{3}{4}$

18. (86) $\frac{2}{3} \times 4$

19. (70) $6.57 + 83¢ + $16

20. (70) 12 × 75¢

Name ______________________________

Score ______________________________

Cumulative Test 20A

Also take **Power-Up Test 20**

1. Which letter names the point at (2, 3)?
(Inv. 8)

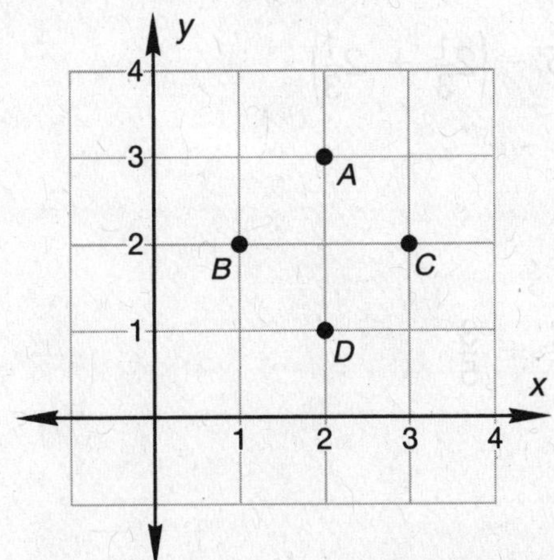

2. A new racket costs $86.50. Mariam has $63.75. How much more money does she need to buy the racket?
(11)

3. Lakeisha has 15 iris bulbs and 25 tulip bulbs in her flower bed. What is the ratio of iris bulbs to tulip bulbs in her flower bed?
(97)

4. The grasshopper jumped 25 cm. How many millimeters is that?
(74)

5. *AB* is 2.7 cm. *BC* is 1.9 cm. *CD* equals *BC*. Find *AD*.
(61, 73)

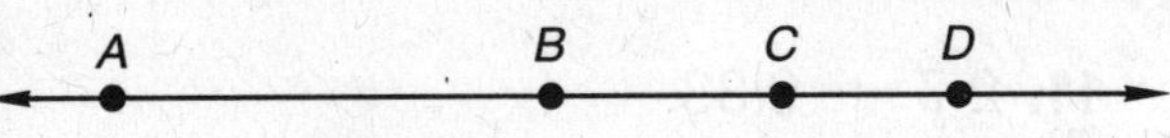

6. **a.** A pint is what fraction of a quart?
(85)
b. A quart is what fraction of a gallon?
c. Use the answers from parts **a** and **b** above to determine what fraction of a gallon a pint represents.

7. Estimate the product of 496 and 351.
(62)

8. Simplify this decimal number:
(100)
0400.203000

9. What is the reciprocal of $\frac{9}{7}$?
(95)

10. (91) Reduce: $4\frac{5}{15}$

11. (99) $2.7 + 0.33 + 4$

12. (78) 2^5

13. (73) $13.459 - 0.36$

14. (70) $20 \times 16¢$

15. (78) $\sqrt{81}$

16. (92) $27\overline{)330}$

17. (24, 63) $5 - \left(2\frac{1}{3} + 2\frac{1}{3}\right)$

18. (96) $\frac{2}{7} \div \frac{3}{5}$

19. (91) $\frac{9}{10} + \frac{7}{10}$

20. (86) $\frac{2}{3} \times 6$

Name ______________________________

Score ______________________________

Cumulative Test 20B

Also take ***Power-Up Test 20***

1. (Inv. 8) Which letter names the point at (3, 2)?

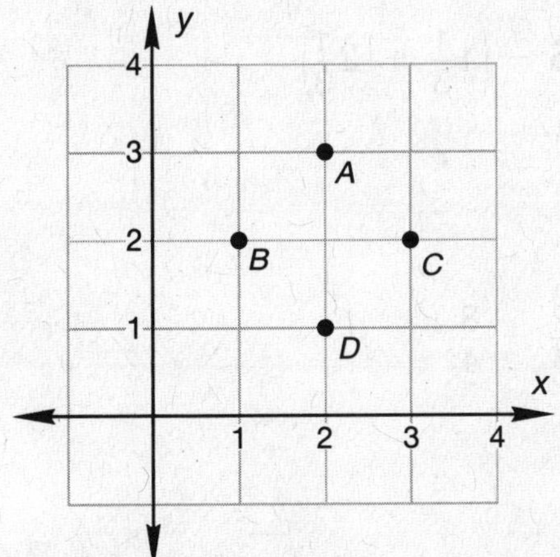

2. (11) A new bat costs \$21.45. Wade has \$16.75. How much more money does he need to buy the bat?

3. (97) There are 18 girls and 12 boys in Ms. Webster's class. What is the ratio of boys to girls in her class?

4. (74) Carl jumped 8 meters. Eight meters is how many centimeters?

5. (61, 73) *AB* is 2.8 cm. *BC* is1.8 cm. *CD* equals *BC*. Find *AD*.

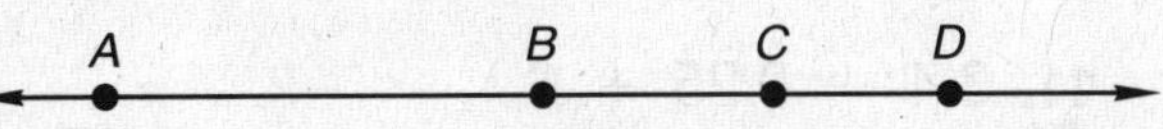

6. (85) **a.** A cup is what fraction of a pint?

b. A pint is what fraction of a quart?

c. Use the answers from part **a** and **b** above to determine what fraction of a quart a cup represents.

7. (62) Estimate the product of 517 and 291.

8. (100) Simplify this decimal number:

005.0700

9. (95) What is the reciprocal of $\frac{7}{5}$?

10. Reduce: $3\frac{8}{12}$
(91)

11. $3.4 + 0.25 + 6$
(99)

12. 2^4
(78)

13. $4.356 - 0.21$
(73)

14. $10 \times 36¢$
(70)

15. $\sqrt{100}$
(78)

16. $23\overline{)500}$
(92)

17. $6 - \left(1\frac{1}{3} + 2\frac{1}{3}\right)$
(24, 63)

18. $\frac{2}{3} \div \frac{3}{4}$
(96)

19. $\frac{5}{8} + \frac{5}{8}$
(91)

20. $\frac{3}{4} \times 2$
(86)

Name ______________________

Score ______________________

Cumulative Test 21A

Also take **Power-Up Test 21**

1. Round \$48.91 to the nearest dollar.
(104)

2. a. Round 9.671 to the nearest whole number.
(101, 104)

b. Round $7\frac{2}{3}$ to the nearest whole number.

3. Arrange these numbers in order from least to greatest: 0.1, 2, and $\frac{2}{3}$.
(69)

4. Two thirds of the 18 cars were new. How many cars were new?
(46)

5. The length of $\overline{AD}$ is 6.4 cm. The length of $\overline{AB}$ is 3.9 cm. The length of $\overline{BC}$ is 1.4 cm. Find the length of $\overline{CD}$.
(61)

6. A shoe box has the shape of what geometric solid?
(83)

7. Which of these angles could measure 120°?
(Inv. 10)

A.

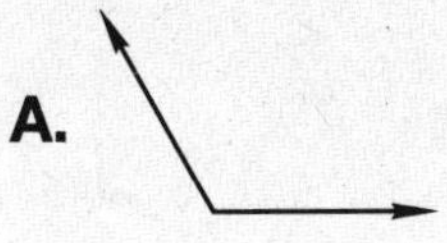

B.

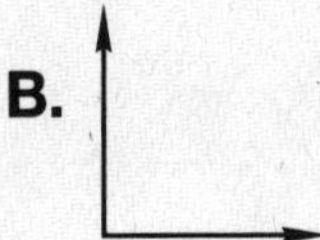

C.

8. 4.39 + 1.8 + 3
(99)

9. 9.14 − 0.8
(73)

10. $2 - 0.8$
(102)

11. 309×14
(51)

12. $7 - \left(2\frac{5}{6} - \frac{1}{6}\right)$
(63, 90)

13. $4\frac{8}{12} + 3\frac{6}{12}$
(91)

14. $\frac{4028}{4}$
(34)

15. $953 \div 30$
(54)

16. $\frac{1}{5} \div \frac{1}{2}$
(96)

17. $\frac{3}{5} \times 10$
(86, 91)

18. Find the volume of this rectangular solid.
(103)

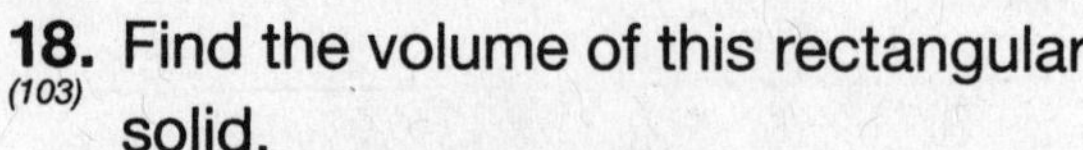

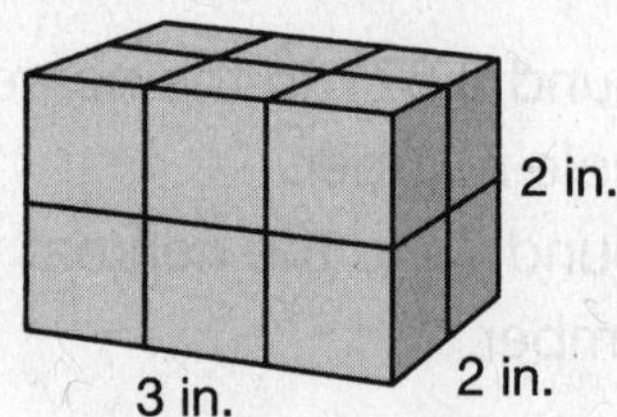

19. Draw an equilateral triangle and show its lines of symmetry.
(105)

20. The denominator of $\frac{11}{12}$ is 12. Write a fraction equal to $\frac{2}{3}$ that also has a denominator of 12 and subtract that fraction from $\frac{11}{12}$. Then reduce the answer.
(79, 90)

Name ______________________________

Score ______________________________

Cumulative Test 21B

Also take **Power-Up Test 21**

1. Round $16.32 to the nearest dollar.
(104)

2. a. Round 12.8 to the nearest whole number.
(101, 104)

b. Round $5\frac{1}{3}$ to the nearest whole number.

3. Arrange these numbers in order from least to greatest: 0.1, 1, and 0.
(69)

4. Four fifths of the 30 students finished the test early. How many students finished the test early?
(46)

5. The length of $\overline{AD}$ is 5.8 cm. The length of $\overline{AB}$ is 3 cm. The length of $\overline{BC}$ is 1.6 cm. Find the length of $\overline{CD}$.
(61)

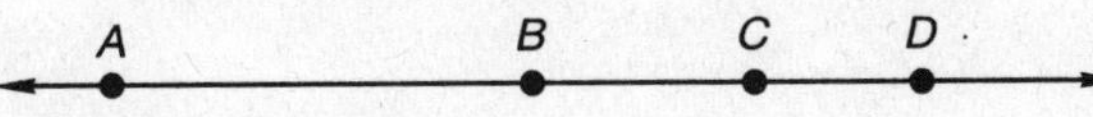

6. A can of tomatoes has the shape of what geometric solid?
(83)

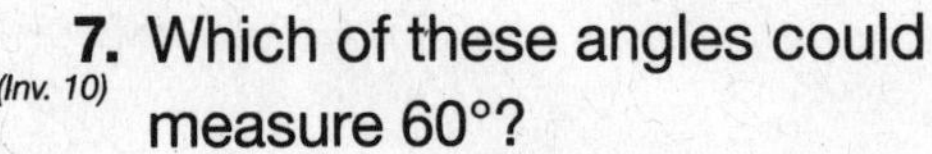

7. Which of these angles could measure 60°?
(Inv. 10)

A.

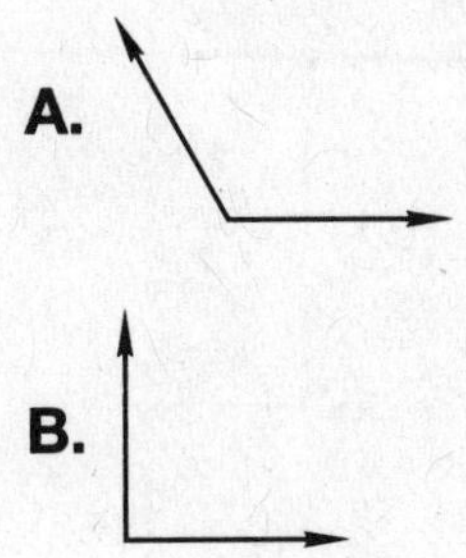

B.

C.

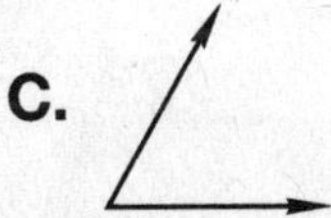

8. 6.25 + 1.4 + 2
(99)

9. 4.23 − 0.4
(73)

10. $3 - 1.2$
(102)

11. 365×12
(51)

12. $6 - \left(3\frac{3}{4} - \frac{1}{4}\right)$
(63, 90)

13. $3\frac{5}{6} + 1\frac{4}{6}$
(91)

14. $\frac{6012}{6}$
(34)

15. $364 \div 20$
(54)

16. $\frac{1}{3} \div \frac{1}{2}$
(96)

17. $\frac{2}{3} \times 3$
(86, 91)

18. Find the volume of this rectangular solid.
(103)

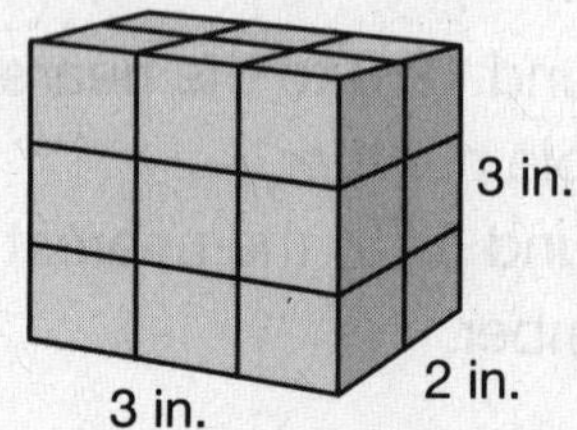

19. Draw a rectangle that is not a square and show its lines of symmetry.
(105)

20. The denominator of $\frac{7}{10}$ is 10. Write a fraction equal to $\frac{1}{2}$ that also has a denominator of 10 and subtract that fraction from $\frac{7}{10}$. Then reduce the answer.
(79, 90)

Name ______________________________

Score ______________________________

Cumulative Test 22A

Also take **Power-Up Test 22**

1. Which digit in 1.3725 is in the thousandths place?
(106)

2. A bolt of cloth is 40 yards long. How many feet long is a bolt of cloth?
(74)

3. Which of these figures has no line of symmetry?
(105)

A. 

B.

C. 

D.

4. There are 7 boys and 14 girls in the class. What is the ratio of boys to girls?
(97)

5. Write 40% as a reduced fraction.
(71, 90)

6. In a roll of 50 dimes, 8 were minted before 1983. What percent of the dimes in the roll were minted before 1983?
(107)

7. Round parts **a** and **b** to the nearest whole number.
(101, 104)

a. $3\frac{2}{7}$

b. 101.496

8. Compare: 1.25 ◯ 12.5
(106)

9. What is the perimeter of this square?
(53)

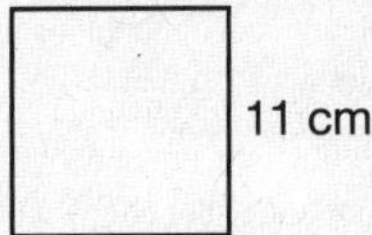

10. What is the area of the square in problem **9**?
(72)

11. (99) $4.76 + 8 + 0.241 + 3.6$

12. (99) $3.4 - 1$

13. (102) $9 - 8.94$

14. (109) 1.7×0.6

15. (110)
$$\begin{array}{r} 0.21 \\ \times\ 0.4 \\ \hline \end{array}$$

16. (63, 90) $3\frac{5}{7} + \left(2 - 1\frac{4}{7}\right)$

17. (86, 91) $\frac{3}{5} \times \left(6 \times \frac{11}{12}\right)$

18. (91) $2\frac{2}{3} + 3\frac{2}{3}$

19. (90, 96) $\frac{6}{7} \div 3$

20. (103) What is the volume of a box of cereal with the dimensions shown?

Name ______________________________

Score ______________________________

Cumulative Test 22B

Also take ***Power-Up Test 22***

1. (106) Which digit in 6.1375 is in the thousandths place?

2. (74) A football field is 100 yards long. How many feet long is a football field?

3. (105) Which of these figures has no line of symmetry?

A. 

B. 

C.

D. 

4. (97) There are 8 girls and 12 boys in the class. What is the ratio of girls to boys?

5. (71, 90) Write 25% as a reduced fraction.

6. (107) In a roll of 50 pennies, 15 were minted before 1985. What percent of the pennies in the roll were minted before 1985?

7. (101, 104) Round parts **a** and **b** to the nearest whole number.

a. $6\frac{5}{8}$

b. 98.631

8. (106) Compare: 0.25 ◯ 0.025

9. (53) What is the perimeter of this square?

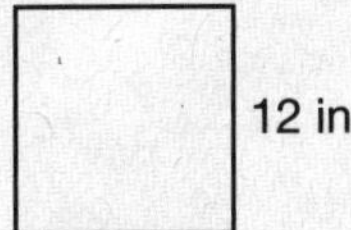

10. (72) What is the area of the square problem **9**?

11. (99) $3.42 + 12 + 0.367 + 5$

12. (99) $2.5 - 1$

13. (102) $5 - 1.36$

14. (109) 1.2×0.3

15. (110)

$$\begin{array}{r} 0.15 \\ \times\ 0.5 \\ \hline \end{array}$$

16. (63, 90) $3\frac{1}{4} + \left(5 - 1\frac{1}{4}\right)$

17. (86, 91) $\frac{3}{4} \times \left(2 \times \frac{2}{3}\right)$

18. (91) $3\frac{3}{4} + 3\frac{3}{4}$

19. (90, 96) $\frac{8}{9} \div 2$

20. (103) What is the volume of a box of cereal with the dimensions shown?

Name ______________________________

Score ______________________________

Cumulative Test 23A

Also take ***Power-Up Test 23***

1. (104) Estimate the sum of 2.42, 3.68, and 14.9 by rounding each number to the nearest whole number before adding.

2. (71) Which of these is not equal to $\frac{1}{5}$?

A. $\frac{4}{20}$ **B.** 20%

C. 0.20 **D.** 0.05

3. (98) What is the temperature shown on this thermometer?

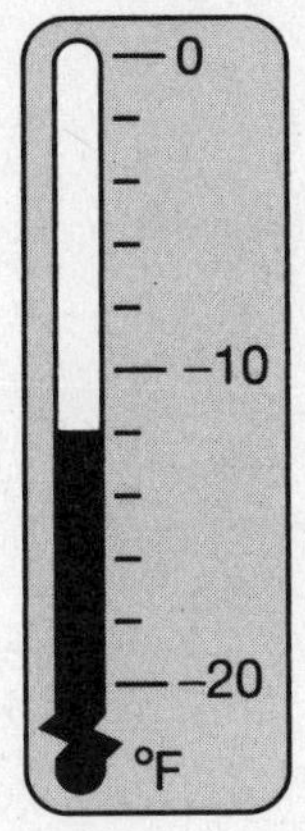

4. (84) What is the mean of 14, 13, 19, and 18?

Use the following graph to answer problems **5** and **6**.

5. (Inv. 8) What letter names the point at (1, 2)?

6. (Inv. 8) Write the coordinates of point *B*.

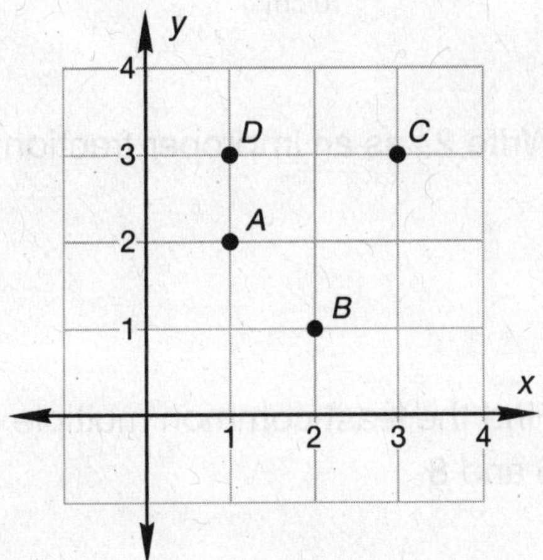

7. (57) The spinner below is divided into 6 congruent sectors. What is the probability that the spinner will stop on an odd number?

8. (53, 115) Refer to the hexagon to answer the following questions. All angles are right angles.

a. What is the perimeter of this hexagon?

b. What is the area of this hexagon?

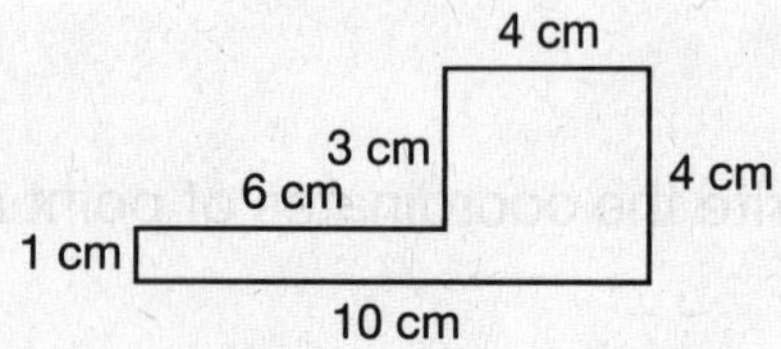

9. (113) Write $2\frac{1}{2}$ as an improper fraction.

10. (112) Find the least common multiple of 6 and 8.

11. (99) $13 + 2.96 + 4.06 + 0.98$

12. (102) $9 - (8.33 - 2.42)$

13. (109) 4.5×9

14. (92) $21\overline{)1390}$

15. (111) 0.2345×1000

16. (110) 0.1×0.02

17. (91) $1\frac{5}{6} + 1\frac{5}{6}$

18. (90) $7\frac{7}{8} - 1\frac{1}{8}$

19. (76, 90) $\frac{4}{5} \times \frac{3}{4}$

20. (96) $\frac{1}{5} \div \frac{3}{10}$

Name ______________________________

Score ______________________________

Also take **Power-Up Test 23**

1. (104) Estimate the sum of 8.16, 7.89, and 8.9 by rounding each number to the nearest whole number before adding.

2. (71) Which of these is not equal to $\frac{1}{2}$?

A. $\frac{5}{10}$ **B.** 0.05

C. 50% **D.** 0.5

3. (98) What is the temperature shown on this thermometer?

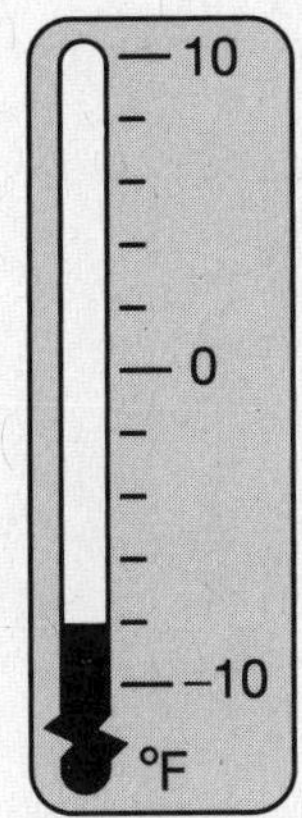

4. (84) What is the mean of 7, 9, 12, 10, and 12?

Use the following graph to answer problems **5** and **6**.

5. (Inv. 8) What letter names the point at (2, 1)?

6. (Inv. 8) Write the coordinates of point *C*.

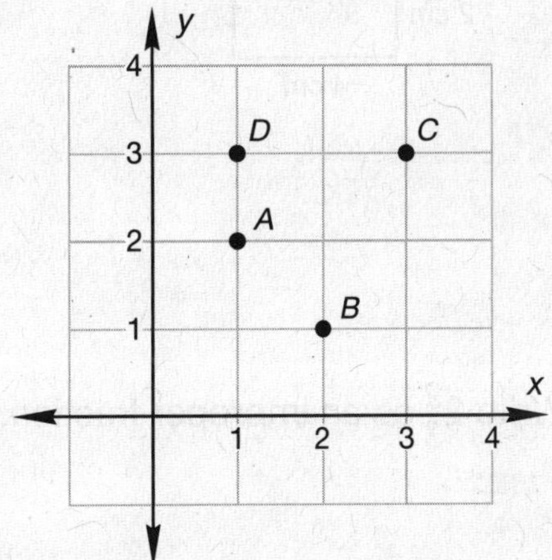

7. (57) The spinner below is divided into 6 congruent sectors. What is the probability that the spinner will stop on an even number?

8. (53, 115) Refer to the hexagon to answer the following questions. All angles are right angles.

a. What is the perimeter of this hexagon?

b. What is the area of this hexagon?

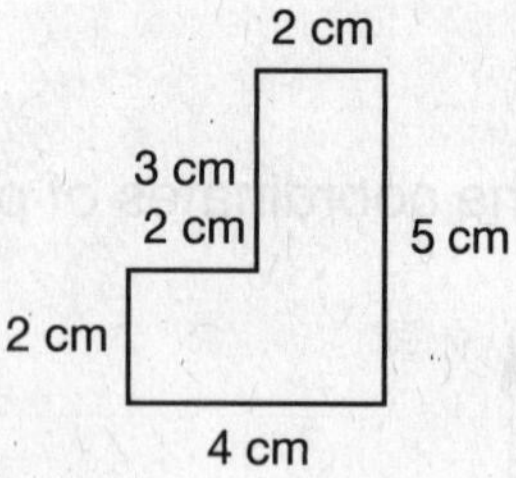

9. (113) Write $2\frac{2}{3}$ as an improper fraction.

10. (112) Find the least common multiple of 6 and 10.

11. (99) $16 + 4.27 + 12 + 0.275$

12. (102) $10 - (5.36 - 2)$

13. (109) 3.6×12

14. (92) $16\overline{)437}$

15. (111) 0.2345×100

16. (110) 0.1×0.01

17. (91) $3\frac{3}{4} + 3\frac{3}{4}$

18. (90) $5\frac{5}{8} - 1\frac{1}{8}$

19. (76, 90) $\frac{5}{6} \times \frac{2}{5}$

20. (96) $\frac{1}{6} \div \frac{1}{8}$

Name ______________________________

Test ______________ Score ______________

Answer Form A

Cumulative Test Solutions

1.	**6.**
2.	**7.**
3.	**8.**
4.	**9.**
5.	**10.**

Answer Form A

11.	16.
12.	17.
13.	18.
14.	19.
15.	20.

Name ______________________________

Test ______________ Score ______________

Answer Form B

Cumulative Test Solutions

1.	**6.**
2.	**7.**
3.	**8.**
4.	**9.**
5.	**10.**

11.	16.
12.	17.
13.	18.
14.	19.
15.	20.

Name ______________________________

Test ______________ Score ______________

Answer Form C

Cumulative Test Solutions

1.	2.	3.	4.
5.	6.	7.	8.
9.	10.	11.	12.
13.	14.	15.	16.
17.	18	19.	20.

1.	
2.	
3.	
4.	
5.	
6.	
7.	
8.	
9.	
10.	
11.	
12.	
13.	
14.	
15.	
16.	
17.	
18.	
19.	
20.	

Class ______________________

Class Test Analysis Form A

Cumulative Tests

Student's Name	Cumulative Test 1	2	3	4
1.				
2.				
3.				
4.				
5.				
6.				
7.				
8.				
9.				
10.				
11.				
12.				
13.				
14.				
15.				
16.				
17.				
18.				
19.				
20.				
21.				
22.				
23.				
24.				
25.				
26.				
27.				
28.				
29.				
30.				

Class ______________________

Class Test Analysis Form A

Cumulative Tests

Student's Name	Cumulative Test 5	Cumulative Test 6	Cumulative Test 7	Cumulative Test 8
1.				
2.				
3.				
4.				
5.				
6.				
7.				
8.				
9.				
10.				
11.				
12.				
13.				
14.				
15.				
16.				
17.				
18.				
19.				
20.				
21.				
22.				
23.				
24.				
25.				
26.				
27.				
28.				
29.				
30.				

Class ______________________

Class Test Analysis Form A

Cumulative Tests

Student's Name	Cumulative Test 9	10	11	12
1.				
2.				
3.				
4.				
5.				
6.				
7.				
8.				
9.				
10.				
11.				
12.				
13.				
14.				
15.				
16.				
17.				
18.				
19.				
20.				
21.				
22.				
23.				
24.				
25.				
26.				
27.				
28.				
29.				
30.				

Class ______________________

Class Test Analysis Form A

Cumulative Tests

Student's Name	Cumulative Test 13	14	15	16
1.				
2.				
3.				
4.				
5.				
6.				
7.				
8.				
9.				
10.				
11.				
12.				
13.				
14.				
15.				
16.				
17.				
18.				
19.				
20.				
21.				
22.				
23.				
24.				
25.				
26.				
27.				
28.				
29.				
30.				

Class ______________________________

Class Test Analysis Form A

Cumulative Tests

Student's Name	Cumulative Test			
	17	18	19	20
1.				
2.				
3.				
4.				
5.				
6.				
7.				
8.				
9.				
10.				
11.				
12.				
13.				
14.				
15.				
16.				
17.				
18.				
19.				
20.				
21.				
22.				
23.				
24.				
25.				
26.				
27.				
28.				
29.				
30.				

Class ____________________

Class Test Analysis Form A

Cumulative Tests

Student's Name	Cumulative Test 21	Cumulative Test 22	Cumulative Test 23
1.			
2.			
3.			
4.			
5.			
6.			
7.			
8.			
9.			
10.			
11.			
12.			
13.			
14.			
15.			
16.			
17.			
18.			
19.			
20.			
21.			
22.			
23.			
24.			
25.			
26.			
27.			
28.			
29.			
30.			

Class ______________________

Individual Test Analysis Form B

Cumulative Tests

Test Item No.	Cumulative Test Number 1	2	3	4	5	6	7	8	9	10	11	12
	Lesson Assessed											
1.	*1*	*11*	*8*	*11*	*25*	*28*	*31*	*35*	*Inv. 4*	*49*	*50*	*57*
2.	*1*	*2*	*15*	*17*	*21*	*13*	*28*	*38*	*Inv. 4*	*48*	*46*	*20*
3.	*1*	*8*	*12*	*6*	*Inv. 2*	*17*	*35*	*32*	*44*	*47*	*35*	*52*
4.	*1*	*7*	*12*	*16*	*Inv. 2*	*21*	*25*	*36*	*43*	*50*	*33*	*52*
5.	*2*	*2*	*14*	*12*	*19*	*2*	*21*	*39*	*45*	*30, 37*	*44, 53*	*50*
6.	*2*	*10*	*11*	*12*	*6*	*2*	*33*	*33*	*40*	*44*	*10*	*53*
7.	*2*	*10*	*11*	*13*	*21*	*7*	*33*	*27*	*44*	*44*	*53*	*53*
8.	*2*	*3*	*12*	*12*	*24*	*27*	*24*	*11*	*30*	*7*	*Inv. 4*	*60*
9.	*3*	*4, 8*	*15*	*2, 15*	*23*	*25*	*30*	*30*	*39*	*13*	*48*	*57*
10.	*3*	*2*	*13*	*17*	*13*	*9*	*30*	*13*	*9*	*13*	*36*	*46*
11.	*3*	*7*	*9*	*17*	*13*	*13*	*31*	*9*	*29*	*17*	*6*	*6*
12.	*3*	*6*	*13*	*9*	*24*	*6*	*27*	*29*	*18*	*29*	*9*	*9*
13.	*4*	*9*	*6*	*13*	*22*	*26*	*13*	*18*	*26*	*9*	*29*	*55*
14.	*4*	*9*	*13*	*18*	*20*	*26*	*13*	*34*	*34*	*34*	*51*	*56*
15.	*4*	*6*	*9*	*20*	*17*	*26*	*18*	*26*	*42*	*26*	*34*	*54*
16.	*4*	*9*	*7*	*20*	*18*	*29*	*29*	*34*	*41*	*34*	*54*	*58*
17.	*5*	*6*	*7*	*20*	*17*	*24*	*34*	*13*	*41*	*41*	*43*	*54*
18.	*5*	*1*	*15*	*18*	*6*	*17*	*26*	*24*	*41*	*41*	*43*	*59*
19.	*5*	*1*	*7*	*14*	*9*	*23*	*34*	*32*	*13, 24*	*41*	*30, 37*	*59*
20.	*5*	*1*	*1*	*10*	*24*	*28*	*32*	*28*	*21*	*Inv. 5*	*52*	*13, 24*

Class ____________________

Individual Test Analysis Form B

Cumulative Tests

Test Item No.	Cumulative Test Number										
	13	**14**	**15**	**16**	**17**	**18**	**19**	**20**	**21**	**22**	**23**
	Lesson Assessed										
1.	50	49	23, 59	49	22, 42	28, 49	95	Inv. 8	104	106	104
2.	60	25	75	78	31, 61	75	79	11	101, 104	74	71
3.	35	67	74	67	31, 61	90	21	97	69	105	98
4.	62	68	68	74	83	85	86	74	46	97	84
5.	33	67	64	77	46	83	71	61, 73	61	71, 90	Inv. 8
6.	31, 61	68	73	64	46	31, 61	69	85	83	107	Inv. 8
7.	38	64	71	79	82	31, 61	66	62	Inv. 10	101, 104	57
8.	57	66	33	79	85	86	91	100	99	106	53, 115
9.	53	69	70	80	81	84	79	95	73	53	113
10.	18	62	58	66	73	79	73	91	102	72	112
11.	41	6	70	70	73	68	9	99	51	99	99
12.	63	9	70	73	78	9	51	78	63, 90	99	102
13.	63	56	73	73	26	56	54	73	91	102	109
14.	9	34	17	54	9	26	78	70	34	109	92
15.	13, 24	18, 29	24, 63	17	56	76	94	78	54	110	111
16.	55	34	59	18, 29	54	78	90	92	96	63, 90	110
17.	34	54	61, 74	26	75	87	91	24, 63	86, 91	86, 91	91
18.	54	24, 63	45	75	24, 63	90	86	96	103	91	90
19.	64	59	53	76	79	90	70	91	105	90, 96	76, 90
20.	58	58	72	61	66, 72	53, 66	70	86	79, 90	103	96

Name ______________________________

Score ______________________________

1. Which digit in 13,679 shows the number of thousands?
(7)

A. 1 **B.** 3 **C.** 6 **D.** 7

2. For a field trip, 120 students will ride on two buses. If 78 students ride on the first bus, then how many students will ride on the second bus?
(16)

A. 32 students **B.** 42 students **C.** 52 students **D.** 62 students

3. 7831 − 4392 equals
(9)

A. 3349 **B.** 4339 **C.** 3439 **D.** 3561

4. \$10.00 − \$2.35 equals
(13)

A. \$8.65 **B.** \$8.35 **C.** \$7.65 **D.** \$7.35

5. What is the rule for the counting sequence below?
(1)

36, 42, 48, 54, . . .

A. Count up by fours. **B.** Count down by sixes.

C. Count up by sixes. **D.** Count up by eights.

6. This table shows how many minutes the students at Hoover Elementary School exercised during PE class. On which day did the students exercise the greatest amount of time?
(4)

Day	Exercise Time
Monday	30 minutes
Tuesday	35 minutes
Wednesday	25 minutes
Thursday	10 minutes
Friday	45 minutes

A. Monday **B.** Tuesday **C.** Wednesday **D.** Friday

7. Luiz is fourth in line. Margie is twelfth in line. How many people are between Luiz and Margie?
(7)

A. 7 people **B.** 8 people **C.** 9 people **D.** 12 people

8. Lisa watched 5 birds land on her feeder. After she added birdseed, more birds landed on the feeder. There were a total of 17 birds on the feeder. How many birds came after Lisa added birdseed?
(11)

A. 5 birds **B.** 8 birds **C.** 11 birds **D.** 12 birds

9. When 15 is subtracted from 33, what is the difference?
(8, 9)

A. 18 **B.** 15 **C.** 8 **D.** 48

10. Lisa, Denzel, and Joshua went fishing. Lisa caught 3 fish and Denzel caught 5 fish. If the friends came home with 9 fish, how many fish did Joshua catch?
(11)

A. 3 fish **B.** 2 fish **C.** 1 fish **D.** 0 fish

11. (7) Which shows how to use digits to write three hundred seventy six thousand, one hundred three?

A. 367,103 **B.** 376,130 **C.** 300,763 **D.** 376,103

12. (4) Train 1 travels 163 miles from Austin to Houston. Train 2 travels 378 miles from Austin to Lubbock. Train three travels 229 miles from Austin to Corpus Christi. Train 4 travels 274 miles from San Antonio to Dallas. Which train traveled the greatest number of miles?

A. Train 1 **B.** Train 2 **C.** Train 3 **D.** Train 4

13. (11) The track team ran 1 mile for a warm-up and 3 miles during practice. How many miles did the team run in all?

A. 2 miles **B.** 3 miles **C.** 4 miles **D.** 5 miles

14. (13) Beth had $7.00 to buy lunch. She spent $3.25 on her lunch. How much does she have left over?

A. $4.75 **B.** $3.75 **C.** $3.25 **D.** $2.25

15. (15) What number is represented by point *M* on this number line?

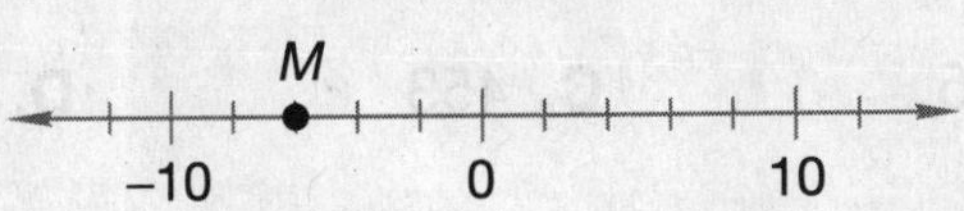

A. –2 **B.** –6 **C.** –4 **D.** –5

16. (17) The product of eighteen and nine is

A. 72 **B.** 189 **C.** 720 **D.** 162

17. (14) Seven years from now Quincy will be 18 years old. How old is Quincy now?

A. 7 years old **B.** 11 years old **C.** 18 years old **D.** 25 y

18. (16) After Jamie emptied 6 gallons of water from the bath tub, there were still 36 gallons left in it. How many gallons of water did Jamie's bathtub hold?

A. 42 gallons **B.** 30 gallons **C.** 40 gallons **D.** 36 gallons

19. (12) In the equation $a + 5 = 20$, what does a equal?

A. 25 **B.** 100 **C.** 10 **D.** 15

20. (13) Which of the following represents $3 + 3 + 3 + 3 + 3 + 3$?

A. 4×3 **B.** 5×3 **C.** 6×3 **D.** 7×3

21. (13) Mira bought a burrito for $1.45, a taco for $1.05 and a beverage for $1.35. The total purchase was

A. $5.20 **B.** $3.85 **C.** $4.60 **D.** $2.60

22. (2) Find the largest three-digit odd number among these choices.

A. 345 **B.** 435 **C.** 453 **D.** 534

23. (6) The sum of 32, 56, 17, 43, and 6 is

A. 144 **B.** 154 **C.** 148 **D.** 208

24. (17) $4.56 × 7 equals

A. $30.92 **B.** $30.52 **C.** $31.92 **D.** $28.52

25. (6) The sum of 1874 and 236 is

A. 2011 **B.** 2000 **C.** 2010 **D.** 2110

Name ______________________________

Score ______________________________

1. Five decades total
(28)

A. 500 years **B.** 50 years **C.** 50 centuries **D.** 5 centuries

2. Which of these shapes is not a polygon?
(32)

A. 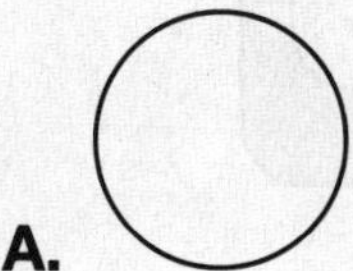 **B.** 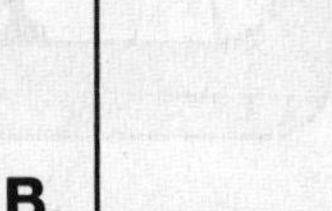 **C.** 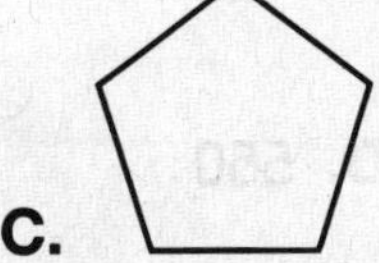 **D.** 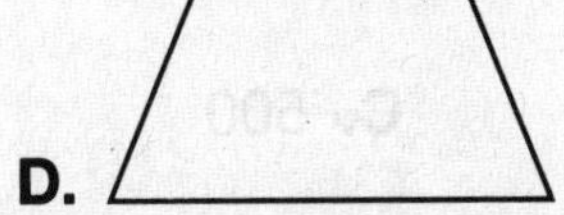

3. The product of eighteen and six is
(17)

A. 24 **B.** 648 **C.** 108 **D.** 3

4. Miguel, Kerry, and Kwan equally shared two dozen blueberries. How many blueberries did each person receive?
(21)

A. 4 **B.** 6 **C.** 8 **D.** 9

5. There were 944 fans in the stadium at Michele's school. Round 944 to the nearest hundred.
(33)

A. 900 **B.** 940 **C.** 950 **D.** 1000

6. Jason reads 23 pages of a book each day. How many pages of the book does Jason read in 5 days?
(21)

A. 75 pages **B.** 85 pages **C.** 115 pages **D.** 123 pages

7. (7) Sam is fourth in line and Celine is seventh. The number of people between Sam and Celine is

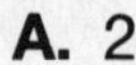

A. 2 **B.** 3 **C.** 4 **D.** 5

8. (27) The arrow appears to be pointing to what number on the scale?

A. 425 **B.** 450

C. 500 **D.** 550

9. (25) Which number is a factor of 32?

A. 64 **B.** 10 **C.** 8 **D.** 3

10. (9) 4352 − 1674 equals

A. 6026 **B.** 2678 **C.** 2778 **D.** 3322

11. (13) \$20.00 − \$7.38 equals

A. \$13.72 **B.** \$13.62 **C.** \$12.62 **D.** \$12.72

12. (35) The planet Uranus was discovered in the year 1781. The planet Neptune was discovered in 1846. How many years were there between the two discoveries?

A. 165 years **B.** 65 years **C.** 3627 years **D.** 85 years

13. (26) The remainder when 436 is divided by 5 is

A. 1 **B.** 2 **C.** 3 **D.** 6

14. Divide: $\frac{300}{5}$
(20, 26)

A. 6 **B.** 60 **C.** 600 **D.** 1500

15. $12.00 ÷ 8 equals
(26)

A. $15.00 **B.** $1.50 **C.** $0.15 **D.** $1.05

16. 40 × 35 equals
(29)

A. 14 **B.** 140 **C.** 1400 **D.** 14,000

17. 6 × (5 + 4) equals
(24)

A. 34 **B.** 15 **C.** 54 **D.** 45

18. Which is the best choice for using compatible numbers to estimate 410 ÷ 7?
(34)

A. 400 ÷ 7 **B.** 420 ÷ 7 **C.** 415 ÷ 7 **D.** 410 ÷ 10

19. If 9*b* = 63, what does *b* equal?
(18)

A. 5 **B.** 6 **C.** 7 **D.** 8

20. Hudson's class starts at 8:30 a.m. and lunch begins at 12:15 p.m. From the time class starts until lunch begins is how many hours and minutes?
(28)

A. 4 hr 15 min **B.** 4 hr 45 min **C.** 3 hr 15 min **D.** 3 hr 45 min

21. Which of these angles appears to be obtuse?
(31)

A. 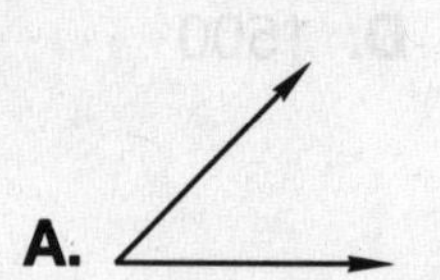
B.
C. 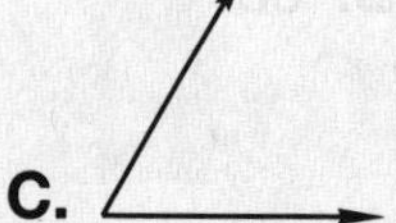
D. 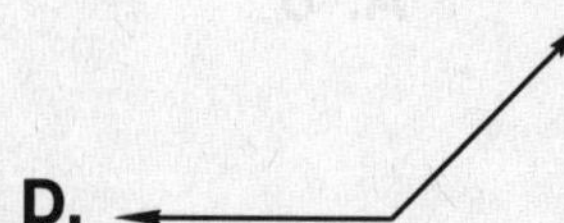

22. The divisor is 7. The dividend is 1253. The quotient is
(26)

A. 189 **B.** 179 **C.** 579 **D.** 879

23. Which fraction does not equal $\frac{1}{2}$?
(23)

A. $\frac{3}{6}$ **B.** $\frac{2}{4}$ **C.** $\frac{2}{2}$ **D.** $\frac{4}{8}$

24. Which of the following numbers is divisible by 2 without a remainder?
(22)

A. 73 **B.** 74 **C.** 77 **D.** 79

25. $7.82 $\times$ 4 equals
(17)

A. $31.28 **B.** $29.28 **C.** $29.12 **D.** $31.12

Name ______________________________

Score ______________________________

1. (57) The face of the spinner is divided into five equal-sized sectors. What is the probability the spinner will stop on a number greater than three?

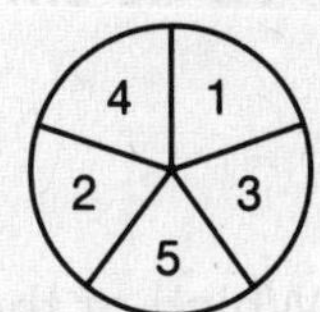

A. $\frac{3}{5}$ **B.** $\frac{2}{5}$ **C.** $\frac{2}{3}$ **D.** $\frac{3}{2}$

2. (20) The divisor is 9. The dividend is 234. The quotient is

A. 2106 **B.** 27 **C.** 26 **D.** 20 R4

3. (52) Twenty million, six hundred seven thousand, twenty-five is

A. 20,600,725 **B.** 20,607,025 **C.** 20,670,025 **D.** 20,600,007,025

4. (52) The digit in the ten-thousands place in 12,345,678 is

A. 1 **B.** 2 **C.** 3 **D.** 4

5. (50) In three stacks of books there are 13 books, 9 books, and 8 books. If the books are rearranged so that each stack has the same number of books, then each stack would have

A. 9 books **B.** 10 books **C.** 11 books **D.** 12 books

6. (53) The perimeter of the triangle is

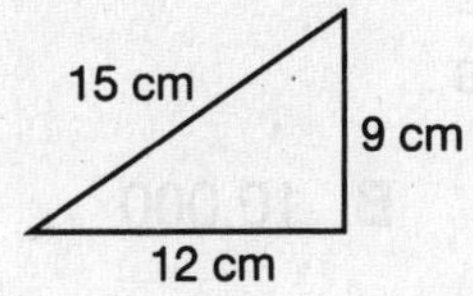

A. 108 cm **B.** 54 cm **C.** 36 cm **D.** 18 cm

7. The radius of a circle is 12 cm. What is its diameter?
(53)

A. 38 cm **B.** 24 cm **C.** 12 cm **D.** 6 cm

8. Which of these numbers is divisible by 9?
(42)

A. 345 **B.** 450 **C.** 652 **D.** 907

9. If the chance of rain is 10%, then rain is
(57)

A. impossible **B.** unlikely **C.** likely **D.** certain

10. Vincent missed $\frac{1}{6}$ of the 30 questions. How many questions did he miss?
(46)

A. 6 **B.** 5 **C.** 4 **D.** 3

11. The sum of 763 and 79 is
(6)

A. 916 **B.** 1442 **C.** 842 **D.** 716

12. 4106 − 1460 equals
(9)

A. 3746 **B.** 3366 **C.** 2646 **D.** 3436

13. 625 × 142 equals
(55)

A. 88,750 **B.** 10,000 **C.** 87,750 **D.** 651,250

14. 405 × 320 equals
(56)

A. 20,250 **B.** 129,600 **C.** 14,400 **D.** 12,960

15. 375 ÷ 10 is between
(54)

A. 36 and 37 **B.** 37 and 38 **C.** 38 and 39 **D.** 374 and 376

16. Which point shows the number $9\frac{1}{6}$?
(38)

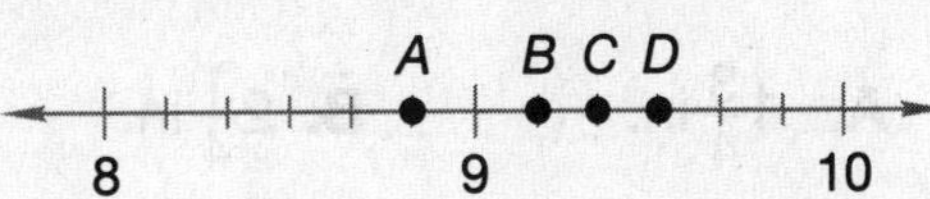

A. Point *A* **B.** Point *B* **C.** Point *C* **D.** Point *D*

17. $6.40 ÷ 20 equals
(54)

A. $3.20 **B.** $0.32 **C.** $3.02 **D.** 3 R20

18. $2\frac{3}{5} + 1\frac{1}{5}$ equals
(41)

A. $3\frac{2}{5}$ **B.** $1\frac{3}{5}$ **C.** $2\frac{4}{5}$ **D.** $3\frac{4}{5}$

19. Matsu cut a piece of string that was 6 feet 9 inches long. How many inches long was the string?
(47)

A. 81 in. **B.** 27 in. **C.** 69 in. **D.** 15 in.

20. $20 − ($3 + $4.75 + $5.49) equals
(13, 24)

A. $13.24 **B.** $7.24 **C.** $27.24 **D.** $6.76

21. Which term best describes this triangle?
(36)

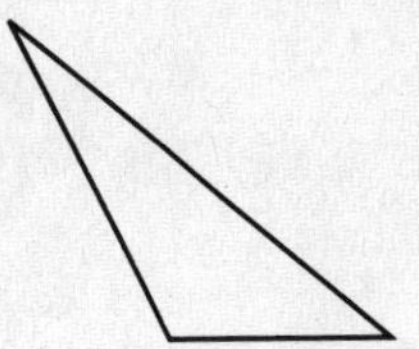

A. right **B.** acute **C.** equilateral **D.** obtuse

22. What is the length of this line segment to the nearest quarter inch?
(44)

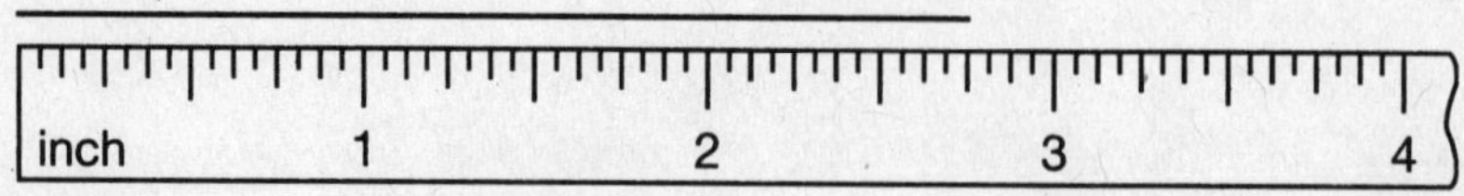

A. $1\frac{3}{4}$ in. B. $2\frac{1}{4}$ in. C. $2\frac{1}{2}$ in. D. $2\frac{3}{4}$ in.

23. Ishmael needs 12 paper cups for his project. If each cup costs $0.12, how much money does Ishmael need?
(51)

A. $12.24 B. $1.12 C. $1.44 D. $144

24. Natasha scored $\frac{1}{4}$ of her basketball team's 24 points. How many points did Natasha score?
(46)

A. 12 points B. 8 points C. 6 points D. 4 points

25. A whole square is 100% of the square. If a square is divided into four equal parts, then each part is what percent of the whole square?
(30, 37)

A. 25% B. 40% C. 50% D. 125%

Name ______________________________

Score ______________________________

1. School starts at 8:30 but Chad wants to arrive 15 minutes early. If the walk to school takes 20 minutes, at what time should he leave home?
(28, 49)

A. 7:50 a.m. **B.** 7:55 a.m. **C.** 8:05 a.m. **D.** 8:10 a.m.

2. The improper fraction $\frac{10}{3}$ equals
(75)

A. $\frac{3}{10}$ **B.** $1\frac{2}{3}$ **C.** $3\frac{1}{3}$ **D.** $3\frac{1}{10}$

3. At the school bake sale, Dupree purchased a brownie for $1.05, a lemon bar for 89¢, and two cookies for $0.45 each. What is a reasonable estimate for the total amount of money he spent?
(62)

A. $2.00 **B.** $3.00 **C.** $4.00 **D.** $5.00

4. Name the shaded portion of this square as a decimal number.
(67)

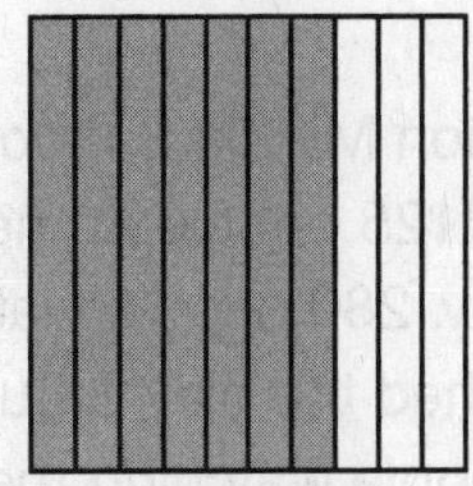

A. 0.3 **B.** 0.4 **C.** 0.7 **D.** 0.10

For problems **5** and **6** refer to quadrilateral *ABCD*.

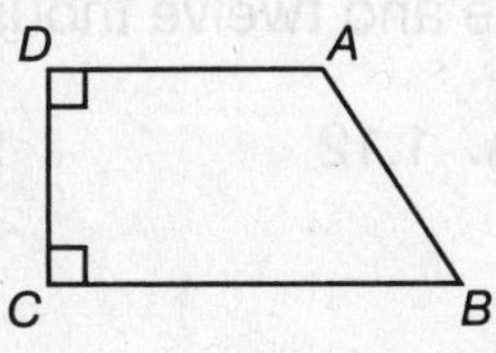

5. The parallel segments are
(31, 61)

A. $\overline{DA}$ and $\overline{DC}$ **B.** $\overline{DA}$ and $\overline{CD}$ **C.** $\overline{DC}$ and $\overline{AB}$ **D.** $\overline{DA}$ and $\overline{CB}$

6. The acute angle is
(31, 61)

A. $\angle A$ B. $\angle B$ C. $\angle C$ D. $\angle D$

7. What is the area of a room that is 12 feet long and 12 feet wide?
(72)

A. 110 sq. ft B. 121 sq. ft C. 144 sq. ft D. 164 sq. ft

8. Ben is 63 inches tall and his younger brother Will is 56 inches tall. How much taller is Ben?
(35)

A. 9 inches B. 8 inches C. 7 inches D. 6 inches

9. 13.02 − 0.65 equals
(73)

A. 12.37 B. 12.67 C. 13.67 D. 13.37

10. Hudson Middle School held a theatre performance. There were 125 people at the dress rehearsal on Thursday. On Friday, 280 people watched the play. Then 175 people watched the play Saturday night. Estimate the total number of people watching the play to the nearest hundred.
(62)

A. 700 people B. 600 people C. 650 people D. 550 people

11. One and twelve thousandths is
(68)

A. 1.12 B. 1.012 C. 0.112 D. 1.1200

12. 34,015 − 3154 equals
(9)

A. 261 B. 31,141 C. 30,861 D. 37,169

13. 360 × 306 equals
(56)

A. 14,760 **B.** 93,636 **C.** 129,600 **D.** 110,160

14. $16.64 ÷ 8 equals
(34)

A. $2.80 **B.** $2.08 **C.** $20.08 **D.** $0.28

15. $\frac{3}{8} \times \frac{1}{2}$ equals
(76)

A. $\frac{3}{16}$ **B.** $\frac{1}{4}$ **C.** $\frac{3}{4}$ **D.** $\frac{4}{10}$

16. Pete's running trail is two and a half kilometers long. How many meters long is Pete's running trail?
(74)

A. 2500 meters **B.** 2200 meters **C.** 1600 meters **D.** 1500 meters

17. Janelle can run around the 4-mile trail with her father in about 36 minutes. About how long does it take Janelle to run one mile?
(21)

A. 6 minutes **B.** 8 minutes **C.** 9 minutes **D.** 12 minutes

18. $1 - \frac{5}{7}$
(77)

A. $\frac{1}{7}$ **B.** $\frac{4}{7}$ **C.** $1\frac{2}{7}$ **D.** $\frac{2}{7}$

19. If four sevenths of the students are boys, then what fraction of the students are girls?
(60)

A. $\frac{3}{7}$ **B.** $\frac{3}{4}$ **C.** $\frac{7}{3}$ **D.** $\frac{7}{4}$

20. The perimeter of this square is
(53, 66)

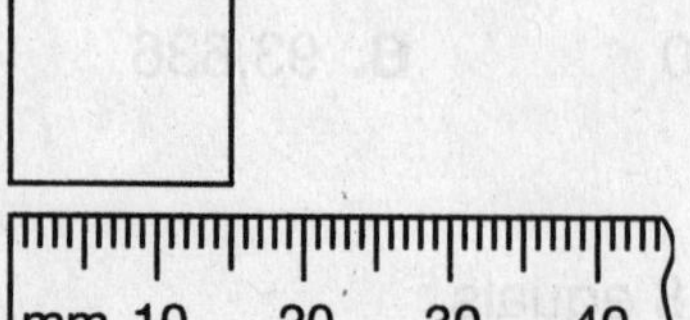

A. 15 mm **B.** 4 cm

C. 30 mm **D.** 6 cm

21. Aaron, Parker, and Denisha will evenly divide 10 cases of fruit juice boxes to hand out to students at lunch. How many cases of fruit juice will each of them have to hand out?
(58)

A. $3\frac{1}{2}$ cases **B.** $3\frac{1}{3}$ cases **C.** $\frac{1}{3}$ cases **D.** 3 cases

22. Use compatible numbers to estimate the sum of $9.76, $6.22, $4.02, and $4.51.
(62)

A. $24.00 **B.** $24.50 **C.** $25.00 **D.** $23.50

23. Which number is greatest: 3.08, 38.0, 0.308, or 308?
(69)

A. 3.08 **B.** 38.0 **C.** 0.308 **D.** 308

24. 8035 ÷ 4 equals
(58)

A. $2008\frac{3}{4}$ **B.** $208\frac{3}{4}$ **C.** $28\frac{3}{4}$ **D.** $20\frac{3}{4}$

25. Jose bought 6 pencils for 60 cents each and a package of dividers for $1.19. How much did he spend altogether?
(80)

A. $4.79 **B.** $1.79 **C.** $10.74 **D.** $1.29

Name ______________________________

Score ______________________________

Benchmark Test 5

For use after Lesson 100

1. Estimate the sum of \$9.95, \$6.20, \$4.15, and \$4.85 by rounding to the nearest dollar before adding.
(62)

A. \$24 **B.** \$25 **C.** \$23 **D.** \$26

2. Leeza had 3 small cakes at her party. The children at the party ate $2\frac{1}{3}$ cakes. How much cake was left over?
(63)

A. $\frac{2}{3}$ cake **B.** $1\frac{1}{2}$ cakes **C.** $2\frac{1}{2}$ cakes **D.** $2\frac{2}{3}$ cakes

3. The fraction $\frac{36}{60}$ equals
(90)

A. $\frac{1}{2}$ **B.** $\frac{3}{5}$ **C.** $\frac{3}{10}$ **D.** $1\frac{2}{5}$

4. Six quarts equals
(85)

A. $1\frac{1}{2}$ gallons **B.** 3 pints **C.** 64 ounces **D.** 3 gallons

5. Which of these numbers is least: 1.002, 28.1, 0.208, or 201?
(69)

A. 1.002 **B.** 28.1 **C.** 201 **D.** 0.208

6. 4^3 equals
(78)

A. $4 + 4 + 4$ **B.** 3×4 **C.** $4 \times 4 \times 4$ **D.** $4 + 3$

7. A tissue box has the shape of a
(83)

A. cylinder **B.** sphere **C.** pyramid **D.** rectangular solid

8. Three fourths of 36 is
(86)

A. 48 B. 27 C. 24 D. 9

9. The median of the ages 11, 10, 16, 10, 13, 10, and 14 is
(84)

A. 6 B. 10 C. 11 D. 12

10. Zack's running trail is 3500 meters long. How many kilometers long is Zack's running trail?
(74)

A. 3.5 kilometers B. 35 kilometers C. 7 kilometers D. 1.75 kilometers

11. Pete can run around the 4 mile trail with his father in about 27 minutes. About how long does it take Pete to run one mile?
(74)

A. 5 minutes B. 6 minutes C. 7 minutes D. 8 minutes

12. Which is a prime number?
(80)

A. 4 B. 6 C. 7 D. 9

13. If $4n = 20$, then what does n^2 equal?
(78)

A. 4 B. 5 C. 16 D. 25

14. What fraction equal to $\frac{1}{2}$ has a denominator 12?
(79)

A. $\frac{3}{12}$ B. $\frac{6}{12}$ C. $\frac{4}{12}$ D. $\frac{2}{12}$

15. Which of these is a composite number?
(80)

A. 9 **B.** 7 **C.** 5 **D.** 3

16. $\sqrt{25} - \sqrt{16}$ equals
(78)

A. 9 **B.** 6 **C.** 3 **D.** 1

17. $\frac{3}{5} \div \frac{3}{5}$ equals
(96)

A. $\frac{9}{25}$ **B.** 1 **C.** $2\frac{4}{25}$ **D.** 3

18. $\frac{15}{16} - \frac{3}{16}$ equals
(41, 90)

A. $\frac{1}{2}$ **B.** 12 **C.** $\frac{3}{4}$ **D.** $\frac{5}{8}$

19. $2\frac{1}{8} + 3\frac{3}{8}$ equals
(90)

A. $5\frac{3}{4}$ **B.** $5\frac{1}{2}$ **C.** $5\frac{7}{8}$ **D.** $6\frac{1}{8}$

20. Which transformation must be used to position triangle *A* on triangle *B*?
(88)

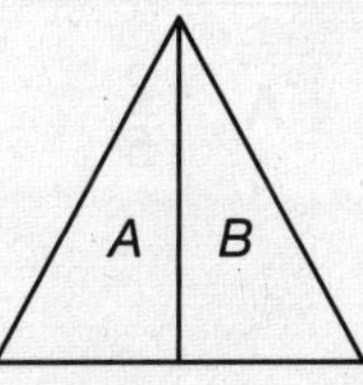

A. rotation **B.** reflection **C.** translation **D.** induction

21. There are 2 grape juice boxes and 4 apple juice boxes in the cooler. If Matt takes one from the cooler without looking, what is the probability that the juice box is grape?
(57, 81)

A. $\frac{1}{2}$ **B.** $\frac{1}{4}$ **C.** $\frac{1}{3}$ **D.** $\frac{1}{6}$

22. Irene has 240 seeds to plant in her garden. There are 8 rows in the garden. How many seeds should Irene put in each row?
(21)

A. 24 seeds **B.** 30 seeds **C.** 40 seeds **D.** 60 seeds

23. It took Tate 117 minutes to read a short story that was 15 pages long. Use compatible numbers to estimate how many minutes it took Tate to read each page.
(94)

A. 8 minutes **B.** 15 minutes **C.** 7 minutes **D.** 17 minutes

24. What is the mode of these data?
(84)
79, 90, 91, 80, 90, 81, 77

A. 90 **B.** 79 **C.** 80.5 **D.** 90.5

25. What is the reciprocal of $\frac{2}{5}$ written as a mixed number?
(95)

A. $1\frac{2}{5}$ **B.** $1\frac{5}{2}$ **C.** $2\frac{1}{2}$ **D.** $2\frac{1}{5}$

Name ______________________________

End-of-Course Exam

Intermediate 5

1. 946 ÷ 22 equals
(92)

A. 430 **B.** 403 **C.** 43 **D.** 4 R 66

2. 6.5 + 2.47 + 0.7 equals
(73)

A. 3.19 **B.** 9.67 **C.** 9.04 **D.** 8.977

3. 23.45 − 1.2 equals
(73)

A. 23.33 **B.** 24.65 **C.** 22.65 **D.** 22.25

4. 75 × 608 equals
(56)

A. 45,600 **B.** 5100 **C.** 56,350 **D.** 52,460

5. $7.20 ÷ 20 equals
(117)

A. $3.60 **B.** $36.00 **C.** $144.00 **D.** 36¢

6. $3\frac{2}{3} + 2\frac{1}{3}$ equals
(41)

A. $5\frac{1}{2}$ **B.** 6 **C.** $1\frac{1}{3}$ **D.** $6\frac{2}{9}$

7. $4\frac{3}{4} - 2\frac{1}{4}$ equals
(81)

A. $2\frac{1}{2}$ **B.** $2\frac{1}{4}$ **C.** $1\frac{1}{2}$ **D.** 7

8. $\frac{3}{5} \times 10$ equals
(86)

A. 2 **B.** 4 **C.** 6 **D.** 8

9. $\frac{3}{4} \div \frac{1}{2}$ equals
(96)

A. $\frac{3}{8}$ B. $1\frac{1}{2}$ C. $\frac{2}{3}$ D. $2\frac{2}{3}$

10. $\frac{8}{12}$ reduces to
(90)

A. $1\frac{1}{2}$ B. $\frac{3}{4}$ C. $\frac{2}{3}$ D. $\frac{1}{4}$

11. Which digit in 125.6 is in the tenths place?
(64)

A. 1 B. 2 C. 5 D. 6

12. Which shows two million, five hundred thousand?
(52)

A. 2,500,000 B. 2,001,500
C. 2,501,000 D. 2,000,500

13. A segment 2 centimeters long is how many millimeters long?
(44)

A. 0.2 millimeters B. 2 millimeters
C. 20 millimeters D. 200 millimeters

14. Which is the best estimate for the width of a classroom door?
(65)

A. 1 kilometer B. 1 meter
C. 1 centimeter D. 1 millimeter

15. Which is not equivalent to $\frac{1}{2}$?
(71)

A. $\frac{2}{4}$ B. 0.5 C. 50% D. 0.2

16. 12^2 equals
(78)

A. 14 B. 24 C. 122 D. 144

17. $\sqrt{100}$ equals
(89)

A. 5^2 **B.** 10^2 **C.** 10 **D.** 50

18. Which shows ten and three tenths?
(68)

A. 10.3 **B.** 10.03 **C.** 0.103 **D.** 103.0

19. Estimate the product of 692 and 412 by rounding each number to the nearest hundred before multiplying?
(62)

A. 240,000 **B.** 280,000
C. 28,000 **D.** 24,000

20. Which group of numbers is in order from least to greatest?
(106)

A. 0.01, 0.1, 1.0 **B.** 0.1, 0.01, 1.0
C. 1.0, 0.1, 0.01 **D.** 0.1, 1.0, 0.01

21. Which is equal to $\frac{1}{3}$?
(79)

A. $\frac{2}{5}$ **B.** $\frac{3}{6}$ **C.** $\frac{3}{9}$ **D.** $\frac{6}{9}$

22. Mike can ride 15 miles in one hour. At that rate, how far can he ride in 3 hours?
(21)

A. 5 miles **B.** 18 miles **C.** 30 miles **D.** 45 miles

23. In three classrooms there were 22, 22, and 25 students. What was the average number of students in the three classrooms?
(50)

A. 22 students **B.** 23 students
C. 24 students **D.** 25 students

24. Kobe's game scores were 85, 80, 80, 85, 80, 90, and 95.
(84)
What is the mode of the scores?

A. 80 B. 85 C. 15 D. 82.5

25. If the arrow is spun, what is the probability
(57)
it will stop in region *A*?

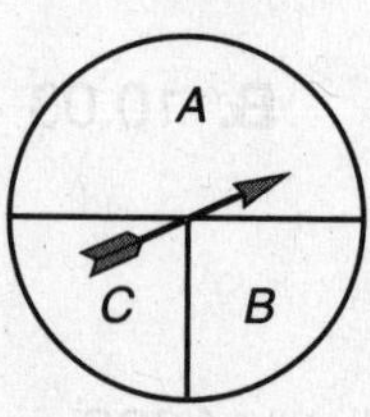

A. $\frac{1}{3}$ B. $\frac{1}{2}$ C. $\frac{1}{4}$ D. $\frac{2}{3}$

26. The meal cost \$5.87. Tax was 49¢. What was the total cost
(70)
including tax?

A. \$5.38 B. \$10.77 C. \$6.36 D. \$54.87

27. The newborn baby weighed 8 pounds. One pound is
(77)
16 ounces. How many ounces is 8 pounds?

A. 128 ounces B. 64 ounces
C. 256 ounces D. 2 ounces

28. Shirts regularly priced at \$27.50 were on sale for half price.
(117)
What was the sale price of a shirt?

A. \$13.25 B. \$13.75 C. \$14.25 D. \$27.00

29. Ling correctly answered 16 of the 20 questions. What fraction
(97)
of the questions did Ling answer correctly?

A. $\frac{1}{5}$ B. $\frac{3}{4}$ C. $\frac{1}{4}$ D. $\frac{4}{5}$

30. At 60 miles per hour, how far can the train travel in 5 hours?
(21)

A. 300 miles
B. 120 miles
C. 3000 miles
D. 12 miles

31. Which triangle does not appear to be a right triangle?
(36)

A.
B.
C.
D.

32. Which angle appears to be an acute angle?
(32)

A.
B.
C.
D.

33. What is the perimeter of the rectangle? Units are in millimeters.
(53)

20 mm
15 mm

A. 35 millimeters
B. 70 millimeters
C. 300 millimeters
D. 75 millimeters

34. The diameter of a wheel is 40 inches. What is the radius of the wheel?
(53)

A. 10 inches
B. 20 inches
C. 80 inches
D. 120 inches

35. What is the area of the rectangle?
(72)

12 in.
8 in.

A. 20 sq. in.
B. 40 sq. in.
C. 96 sq. in.
D. 106 sq. in.

36. What fraction of the circle is shaded?
(30)

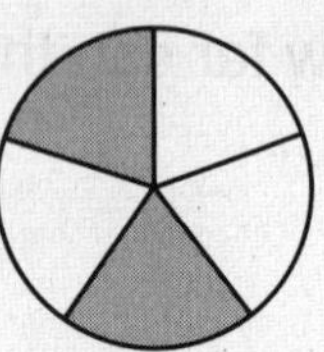

A. $\frac{2}{5}$ **B.** $\frac{2}{3}$ **C.** $\frac{3}{5}$ **D.** $\frac{1}{5}$

37. A cube has how many faces?
(83)

A. 12 **B.** 3 **C.** 6 **D.** 8

38. Which triangle below appears to be congruent to this triangle?
(32)

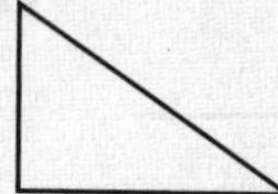

A. 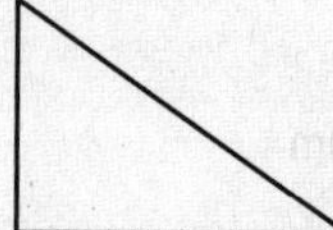 **B.** 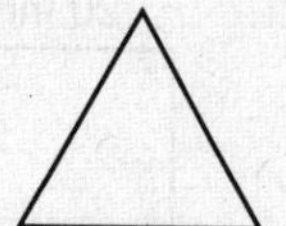 **C.** 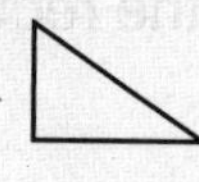 **D.** 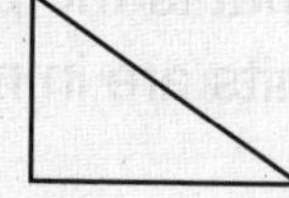

39. Which pair of lines appears to be parallel?
(31)

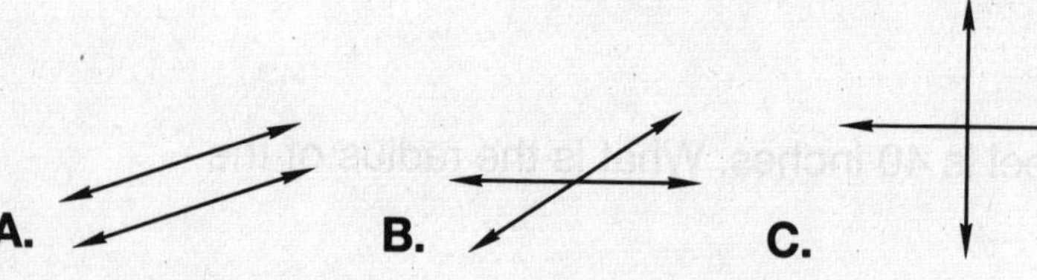

40. The area of the square is 1 square yard. The area is also how many square feet?
(72, 74)

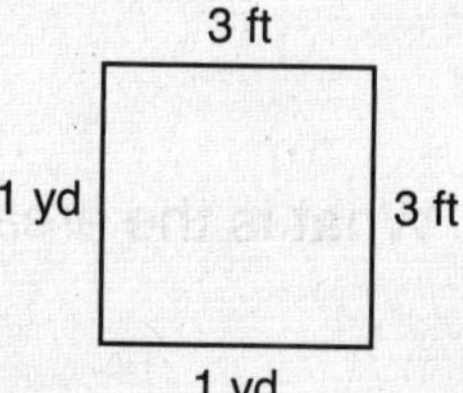

A. 3 sq. ft **B.** 6 sq. ft
C. 9 sq. ft **D.** 12 sq. ft

41. Which comparison is true?
(98)

A. $-5 < -7$ **B.** $-2 < -1$

C. $-3 > 0$ **D.** $2 < -3$

42. If $n - 12 = 15$, then n equals
(14)

A. 27 **B.** 18 **C.** 17 **D.** 3

43. $5\frac{2}{3} - \left(4 - 1\frac{1}{3}\right)$ equals
(41, 63)

A. $\frac{1}{3}$ **B.** $3\frac{2}{3}$ **C.** 4 **D.** 3

44. Which of these numbers is not a factor of 12?
(25)

A. 2 **B.** 3 **C.** 4 **D.** 5

45. Which does not equal 6×12?
(17, 24)

A. $(6 \times 10) + (6 \times 2)$ **B.** $(6 \times 6) + (6 \times 6)$

C. $(6 \times 3) + (6 \times 4)$ **D.** $(3 \times 12) + (3 \times 12)$

46. If $3n = 36$, then n equals
(18)

A. 6 **B.** 9 **C.** 12 **D.** 33

47. Which of the following shows that the product of $\frac{1}{2}$ and $\frac{1}{2}$ is less than the sum of $\frac{1}{2}$ and $\frac{1}{2}$?
(4, 6)

A. $\frac{1}{2} \times \frac{1}{2} < \frac{1}{2} + \frac{1}{2}$ **B.** $\frac{1}{2} \times \frac{1}{2} > \frac{1}{2} + \frac{1}{2}$

C. $\frac{1}{2} - \frac{1}{2} < \frac{1}{2} + \frac{1}{2}$ **D.** $\frac{1}{2} \div \frac{1}{2} < \frac{1}{2} + \frac{1}{2}$

48. If $2x$ equals 12, then $2 + x$ equals
(18)

A. 6 **B.** 8 **C.** 4 **D.** 14

49. Point *A* could represent which of these numbers?
(98)

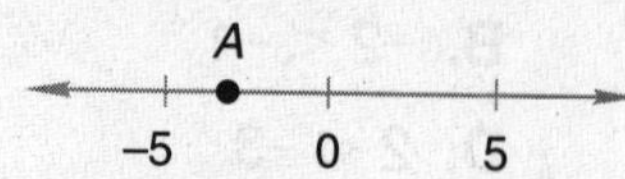

A. $\frac{1}{2}$ **B.** 3 **C.** –3 **D.** –8

50. Which point has the coordinates (3, 2)?
(Inv. 8)

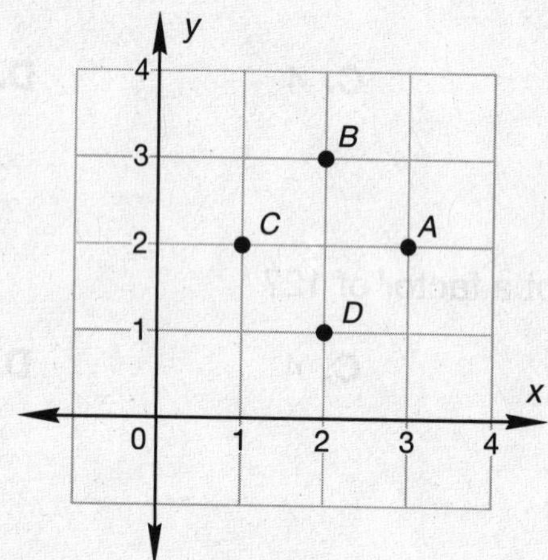

A. Point *A*

B. Point *B*

C. Point *C*

D. Point *D*

Baseline Test

1. **C.** 15
2. **C.** hundreds
3. **D.** 34
4. **A.** $765
5. **B.** $24
6. **C.** 6
7. **B.** 20 cm
8. **C.** arrow *C*
9. **A.**
10. **B.** $\frac{1}{4}$
11. **B.** 15 sq. cm
12. **A.** 12,540,000
13. **C.** 56
14. **D.** $1\frac{3}{4}$ in.
15. **B.** 4 quarts
16. **A.** $3.62
17. **C.** 6
18. **B.** $175
19. **D.** 48 eggs
20. **A.** 16.15
21. **C.** 30 minutes
22. **D.** 5300
23. **D.** 5
24. **A.** $\frac{1}{2} > \frac{1}{4}$
25. **D.** 180 mi
26. **B.** 2000
27. **A.** $\frac{2}{5}$
28. **C.** 64
29. **B.** hexagon
30. **D.** 24
31. **B.** 20 mm
32. **A.** 1 kilogram
33. **C.** 
34. **B.** 205
35. **A.** 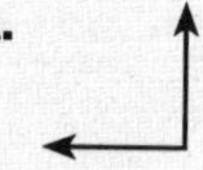
36. **B.** $0.73
37. **C.** $360.00
38. **D.** 972
39. **C.** parallelogram
40. **B.** 8 students
41. **B.** 90
42. **C.** 85
43. **A.** cylinder
44. **B.** $\frac{1}{6}$
45. **A.** 45
46. **D.** $\frac{4}{9}$
47. **C.** $\frac{5}{7}$
48. **A.** $\frac{3}{4}$
49. **B.** 92
50. **C.** $\frac{3}{4}$

Facts Add.

5 + 5 10	2 + 9 11	4 + 5 9	3 + 7 10	8 + 8 16	2 + 6 8	6 + 9 15	4 + 8 12	2 + 4 6	7 + 9 16
3 + 4 7	7 + 8 15	5 + 9 14	2 + 3 5	4 + 9 13	6 + 6 12	5 + 0 5	3 + 8 11	10 + 10 20	5 + 6 11
0 + 0 0	2 + 7 9	9 + 9 18	5 + 7 12	3 + 3 6	4 + 6 10	2 + 2 4	9 + 1 10	8 + 9 17	3 + 6 9
4 + 4 8	3 + 9 12	2 + 5 7	6 + 8 14	7 + 7 14	3 + 5 8	5 + 8 13	4 + 7 11	2 + 8 10	6 + 7 13

Problem Solving Answer the question below.

Problem: Josh purchased a snack bar from the vending machine for 75¢. He used 7 coins. As Josh inserted the coins into the machine, the display counted up as follows: 10¢, 35¢, 45¢, 50¢, 60¢, 65¢, 75¢. What coins did Josh use to purchase the snack bar? 1 quarter, 4 dimes, 2 nickels

Understand

Jose used 7 coins with a total value of 75¢
Display counts up 10¢, 35¢, 45¢, 50¢, 60¢, 65¢, 75¢.
I am asked to find the coins.

Plan

I will use the pattern of counting up to find the coins.

Solve

To get the first value of 10¢, I need a dime.
To go from 10¢ to 35¢, I need a quarter.
To go from 35¢ to 45¢, I need a dime.
To go from 45¢ to 50¢, I need a nickel.
To go from 50¢ to 60¢, I need a dime.
To go from 60¢ to 65¢, I need a nickel.
To go from 65¢ to 75¢, I need a dime.

Altogether, Josh used **1 quarter, 4 dimes,** and **2 nickels.**

Check

My answer is reasonable because 1 quarter, 4 dimes, and 2 nickels is 7 coins altogether, and the total value is 25¢ + 10¢ + 10¢ + 10¢ + 10¢ + 5¢ + 5¢ = 75¢.

Answers

Power-Up Test 2

Facts

Add.

5 + 5 10	2 + 9 11	4 + 5 9	3 + 7 10	8 + 8 16	2 + 6 8	6 + 9 15	4 + 8 12	2 + 4 6	7 + 9 16
3 + 4 7	7 + 8 15	5 + 9 14	2 + 3 5	4 + 9 13	6 + 6 12	5 + 0 5	3 + 8 11	10 + 10 20	5 + 6 11
0 + 0 0	2 + 7 9	9 + 9 18	5 + 7 12	3 + 3 6	4 + 6 10	2 + 2 4	9 + 1 10	8 + 9 17	3 + 6 9
4 + 4 8	3 + 9 12	2 + 5 7	6 + 8 14	7 + 7 14	3 + 5 8	5 + 8 13	4 + 7 11	2 + 8 10	6 + 7 13

Problem Solving

Answer the question below.

Problem: Matt, Clint, and Brian take turns playing pitcher for the baseball team. Matt pitched in the first game, Clint pitched in the second game, and Brian pitched in the third game. For the fourth game, Matt pitched again. If the players continue taking the same order of turns as pitcher, who will pitch in the ninth game? Brian

Understand

Matt, Clint, and Brian take turns pitching.
The pattern is Matt, Clint, Brian, Matt…
I am asked to find which player will pitch in the ninth game.

Plan

I can continue the pattern to find who pitched in the ninth game.

Solve

Game	1	2	3	4	5	6	7	8	9
Pitcher	Matt	Clint	Brian	Matt	Clint	Brian	Matt	Clint	Brian

Brian will pitch in the ninth game.

OR

I know that the pattern starts over with Matt at Game 4, Game 7, and Game 10. Since Matt pitches in the tenth game, I know that **Brian** pitches in the ninth game.

Check

My answer is reasonable because it follows the pattern of "Matt, Clint, Brian."

Facts Subtract.

9 − 8 = 1	8 − 5 = 3	16 − 9 = 7	11 − 9 = 2	9 − 3 = 6	12 − 4 = 8	14 − 9 = 5	6 − 4 = 2	16 − 8 = 8	5 − 2 = 3
14 − 7 = 7	20 − 10 = 10	10 − 7 = 3	15 − 6 = 9	13 − 7 = 6	18 − 9 = 9	10 − 8 = 2	7 − 3 = 4	11 − 5 = 6	9 − 4 = 5
12 − 6 = 6	10 − 5 = 5	17 − 9 = 8	13 − 8 = 5	12 − 3 = 9	7 − 2 = 5	14 − 8 = 6	8 − 6 = 2	15 − 7 = 8	13 − 9 = 4
8 − 4 = 4	12 − 5 = 7	9 − 2 = 7	16 − 7 = 9	11 − 8 = 3	6 − 3 = 3	10 − 6 = 4	17 − 8 = 9	10 − 10 = 0	11 − 4 = 7

Problem Solving Answer the question below.

Problem: Coins are often put into paper or plastic rolls to make their values easier to calculate. Nickels are put into rolls of 40 nickels. Pennies are put into rolls of 50 pennies. What is the value of two rolls of nickels? Two rolls of nickels have the same value as how many rolls of pennies? Two rolls of nickels: $4; 8 rolls of pennies

Understand

40 nickels in a roll
50 pennies in a roll
I am asked to find the value of two rolls of nickels and how many rolls of pennies equal this value.

Plan

I will write equations.

Solve

One roll of nickels: 40 × 5¢ = 200¢ or $2

One roll of nickels is $2, so 2 rolls of nickels is 2 × $2 = **$4.**

One roll of pennies is 50¢, so 2 rolls of pennies have a value of $1.

So $4 is 4 × 2 rolls = **8 rolls of pennies.**

Check

My answers are reasonable because 80 nickels have a value of 80 × 5¢ = 400¢ or $4.
Also, 8 rolls of pennies have a value of 8 × 50¢ = 400¢ or $4.

Answers

Power-Up Test 4

Facts Multiply.

9 × 6 = 54	7 × 1 = 7	9 × 2 = 18	10 × 10 = 100	7 × 4 = 28	6 × 5 = 30	3 × 2 = 6	4 × 4 = 16	8 × 6 = 48	6 × 3 = 18
7 × 7 = 49	4 × 3 = 12	8 × 5 = 40	2 × 2 = 4	9 × 9 = 81	8 × 3 = 24	3 × 0 = 0	9 × 7 = 63	7 × 2 = 14	8 × 8 = 64
5 × 4 = 20	6 × 2 = 12	6 × 6 = 36	7 × 3 = 21	5 × 5 = 25	8 × 7 = 56	3 × 3 = 9	9 × 8 = 72	4 × 2 = 8	0 × 7 = 0
9 × 4 = 36	9 × 5 = 45	8 × 2 = 16	6 × 4 = 24	9 × 3 = 27	5 × 2 = 10	8 × 4 = 32	7 × 5 = 35	5 × 3 = 15	7 × 6 = 42

Problem Solving Answer the question below.

Problem: Mae-Lin has three drawers for storing clothes: a top drawer, a middle drawer, and a bottom drawer. Mae-Lin wants to put her socks in one drawer, her T-shirts in another drawer, and her jeans in another drawer. How many ways can Mae-Lin store her clothes if she puts her socks in the bottom drawer? Use diagrams to show all the ways. 2 ways

Understand

3 drawers: top, middle, bottom

Socks will go in bottom drawer.

I am asked to find how many ways the clothes can go in the drawers. I am also asked to use diagrams to show the ways.

Plan

I will draw diagrams.

Solve

Way 1	Way 2
T-shirts	jeans
jeans	T-shirts
socks	socks

There are 2 ways that Mae-Lin can store her clothes.

Check

My answers are reasonable because each way shows an arrangement of the clothes with the socks at the bottom.

Facts Add.

5 + 5 = 10	2 + 9 = 11	4 + 5 = 9	3 + 7 = 10	8 + 8 = 16	2 + 6 = 8	6 + 9 = 15	4 + 8 = 12	2 + 4 = 6	7 + 9 = 16
3 + 4 = 7	7 + 8 = 15	5 + 9 = 14	2 + 3 = 5	4 + 9 = 13	6 + 6 = 12	5 + 0 = 5	3 + 8 = 11	10 + 10 = 20	5 + 6 = 11
0 + 0 = 0	2 + 7 = 9	9 + 9 = 18	5 + 7 = 12	3 + 3 = 6	4 + 6 = 10	2 + 2 = 4	9 + 1 = 10	8 + 9 = 17	3 + 6 = 9
4 + 4 = 8	3 + 9 = 12	2 + 5 = 7	6 + 8 = 14	7 + 7 = 14	3 + 5 = 8	5 + 8 = 13	4 + 7 = 11	2 + 8 = 10	6 + 7 = 13

Problem Solving Answer the question below.

Problem: Tonight Sharise will use her telescope to observe Mars, Jupiter, and Saturn, though not necessarily in that order. What are the possible orders she can look at the three planets? (Use the abbreviations M for Mars, J for Jupiter, and S for Saturn to list the possible orders.) M-J-S; M-S-J; J-M-S; J-S-M; S-M-J; S-J-M

Understand

Sharise will look at Mars, Jupiter, Saturn, but not necessarily in that order.
I am asked to list the possible orders the planets can be observed, using the abbreviations M, J, and S.

Plan

I will make an organized list. I will list the orders that begin with M, then the orders that begin with J, and then the orders that begin with S.

Solve

Begin with M	Begin with J	Begin with S
M-J-S	J-M-S	S-M-J
M-S-J	J-S-M	S-J-M

The possible orders of observation are M-J-S, M-S-J, J-M-S, J-S-M, S-M-J, and S-J-M.

Check

My answers are reasonable because each order contains each of the three planets.
I found all the orders by making an organized list.

Answers

Power-Up Test 6

Facts

Subtract.

9 − 8 = 1	8 − 5 = 3	16 − 9 = 7	11 − 9 = 2	9 − 3 = 6	12 − 4 = 8	14 − 9 = 5	6 − 4 = 2	16 − 8 = 8	5 − 2 = 3
14 − 7 = 7	20 − 10 = 10	10 − 7 = 3	15 − 6 = 9	13 − 7 = 6	18 − 9 = 9	10 − 8 = 2	7 − 3 = 4	11 − 5 = 6	9 − 4 = 5
12 − 6 = 6	10 − 5 = 5	17 − 9 = 8	13 − 8 = 5	12 − 3 = 9	7 − 2 = 5	14 − 8 = 6	8 − 6 = 2	15 − 7 = 8	13 − 9 = 4
8 − 4 = 4	12 − 5 = 7	9 − 2 = 7	16 − 7 = 9	11 − 8 = 3	6 − 3 = 3	10 − 6 = 4	17 − 8 = 9	10 − 10 = 0	11 − 4 = 7

Problem Solving

Answer the question below.

Problem: Half of the students on the playground were playing soccer. Half of the soccer players were girls. Half of the girls playing soccer wore red shirts. If there were 3 soccer-playing girls who wore red shirts, how many students were on the playground altogether? 24 students

Understand

Half of the students on the playground were playing soccer.
Half of the soccer players were girls.
Half of the girls playing soccer wore red shirts.
There were 3 soccer-playing girls who wore red shirts.
I am asked to find how many students were on the playground altogether.

Plan

I will first find how many girls were playing soccer. Then I will use that number to find how many students played soccer. Then I will use that number to find the total number of students.

Solve

3 is half of 6, so there were 6 girls playing soccer.
6 is half of 12, so there were 12 students playing soccer.
12 is half of 24, so there were **24 students** on the playground.

Check

My answer is reasonable because half of 24 is 12, half of 12 is 6, and half of 6 is 3, which is the number of soccer-playing girls who wore red shirts.

Facts Subtract.

9 − 8 = 1	8 − 5 = 3	16 − 9 = 7	11 − 9 = 2	9 − 3 = 6	12 − 4 = 8	14 − 9 = 5	6 − 4 = 2	16 − 8 = 8	5 − 2 = 3
14 − 7 = 7	20 − 10 = 10	10 − 7 = 3	15 − 6 = 9	13 − 7 = 6	18 − 9 = 9	10 − 8 = 2	7 − 3 = 4	11 − 5 = 6	9 − 4 = 5
12 − 6 = 6	10 − 5 = 5	17 − 9 = 8	13 − 8 = 5	12 − 3 = 9	7 − 2 = 5	14 − 8 = 6	8 − 6 = 2	15 − 7 = 8	13 − 9 = 4
8 − 4 = 4	12 − 5 = 7	9 − 2 = 7	16 − 7 = 9	11 − 8 = 3	6 − 3 = 3	10 − 6 = 4	17 − 8 = 9	10 − 10 = 0	11 − 4 = 7

Problem Solving Answer the question below.

Problem: Darrin, Jennifer, and Jack lined up to get on the bus. Jennifer stood right behind Jack. Darrin was not at the front of the line. In what order did the children line up? Jack, Jennifer, Darrin

Understand

Darrin, Jennifer, and Jack lined up. Jennifer stood right behind Jack. Darrin was not at the front of the line.

I am asked to find the order in which the children lined up.

Plan

I will use logical reasoning to answer the question.

Solve

The first person in line is not Darrin, so it must be either Jennifer or Jack. We are told that Jennifer stood right behind Jack, so the order must be **Jack, Jennifer, Darrin.**

Check

My answer is reasonable because Darrin is not first in line and because Jennifer is right behind Jack.

Power-Up Test 8

Facts

Multiply.

$9 \times 6 = 54$	$7 \times 1 = 7$	$9 \times 2 = 18$	$10 \times 10 = 100$	$7 \times 4 = 28$	$6 \times 5 = 30$	$3 \times 2 = 6$	$4 \times 4 = 16$	$8 \times 6 = 48$	$6 \times 3 = 18$
$7 \times 7 = 49$	$4 \times 3 = 12$	$8 \times 5 = 40$	$2 \times 2 = 4$	$9 \times 9 = 81$	$8 \times 3 = 24$	$3 \times 0 = 0$	$9 \times 7 = 63$	$7 \times 2 = 14$	$8 \times 8 = 64$
$5 \times 4 = 20$	$6 \times 2 = 12$	$6 \times 6 = 36$	$7 \times 3 = 21$	$5 \times 5 = 25$	$8 \times 7 = 56$	$3 \times 3 = 9$	$9 \times 8 = 72$	$4 \times 2 = 8$	$0 \times 7 = 0$
$9 \times 4 = 36$	$9 \times 5 = 45$	$8 \times 2 = 16$	$6 \times 4 = 24$	$9 \times 3 = 27$	$5 \times 2 = 10$	$8 \times 4 = 32$	$7 \times 5 = 35$	$5 \times 3 = 15$	$7 \times 6 = 42$

Problem Solving

Answer the question below.

Problem: Each package of balloons contains exactly 4 red balloons, 3 white balloons, and 3 blue balloons. Allen purchased 2 packages of balloons for party decorations. If he wants to use an equal number of each color, what is the greatest number of balloons Allen can use at the party? How many balloons of each color will he use? 18 balloons; 6 of each color

Understand

Each package: 4 red, 3 white, 3 blue
2 packages
Allen will use an equal number of each color.
I am asked to find the greatest number of balloons Allen can use.

Plan

I will first find the number of each color in 2 packages. The color with the least number of balloons is the amount that can be used.

Solve

1 package: 4 red, 3 white, 3 blue
2 packages: 8 red, 6 white, 6 blue
Allen can use **18 balloons**. He can use **6 balloons of each color.**

Check

My answer is reasonable, because 2 packages contain only 6 white and 6 blue balloons. There will be 2 red balloons left over.

Facts Divide.

7 7)49	5 5)25	9 3)27	8 3)24	1 9)9	4 3)12	4 4)16	5 2)10	7 6)42	7 4)28
0 6)0	2 2)4	7 5)35	3 2)6	5 3)15	9 6)54	8 2)16	9 8)72	6 5)30	7 3)21
3 3)9	9 9)81	8 5)40	5 4)20	8 7)56	9 2)18	6 6)36	7 8)56	6 2)12	6 7)42
8 6)48	7 2)14	9 4)36	6 4)24	9 5)45	4 2)8	6 3)18	9 7)63	8 4)32	8 8)64

Problem Solving Answer the question below.

Problem: Jessica will roll two dot cubes. She needs to roll a total of 9 on the cubes to win the board game. Copy and complete this table to show the ways Jessica can roll a total of 9 on two dot cubes.

1st Cube	2nd Cube

Understand

2 dot cubes
Total of 9 on the cubes
I am asked to complete a table to show the ways to roll 9 with two dot cubes.

Plan

I will complete the table.

Solve

1st Cube	2nd Cube
3	6
4	5
5	4
6	3

Check

My answers are reasonable because the total in each row is 9. Each pair contains numbers from 1 to 6, since those are the numbers on dot cubes.

Answers

Power-Up Test 10

Facts Multiply.

$9 \times 6 = 54$	$7 \times 1 = 7$	$9 \times 2 = 18$	$10 \times 10 = 100$	$7 \times 4 = 28$	$6 \times 5 = 30$	$3 \times 2 = 6$	$4 \times 4 = 16$	$8 \times 6 = 48$	$6 \times 3 = 18$
$7 \times 7 = 49$	$4 \times 3 = 12$	$8 \times 5 = 40$	$2 \times 2 = 4$	$9 \times 9 = 81$	$8 \times 3 = 24$	$3 \times 0 = 0$	$9 \times 7 = 63$	$7 \times 2 = 14$	$8 \times 8 = 64$
$5 \times 4 = 20$	$6 \times 2 = 12$	$6 \times 6 = 36$	$7 \times 3 = 21$	$5 \times 5 = 25$	$8 \times 7 = 56$	$3 \times 3 = 9$	$9 \times 8 = 72$	$4 \times 2 = 8$	$0 \times 7 = 0$
$9 \times 4 = 36$	$9 \times 5 = 45$	$8 \times 2 = 16$	$6 \times 4 = 24$	$9 \times 3 = 27$	$5 \times 2 = 10$	$8 \times 4 = 32$	$7 \times 5 = 35$	$5 \times 3 = 15$	$7 \times 6 = 42$

Problem Solving Answer the question below.

Problem: Ms. Sund will arrange 16 desks into equal-length rows. She will make at least 2 rows, and each row will contain at least 4 desks. How many different arrangements of desks can Ms. Sund make? List or draw the arrangements.

2 arrangements; 4 rows of 4 desks; 2 rows of 8 desks

Understand

16 desks
At least 2 rows.
Each equal-length row will contain at least 4 desks.
I am asked to find how many different arrangements can be made. I am also asked to list or draw the arrangements.

Plan

I will draw diagrams.

Solve

```
□□□□    □□□□□□□□
□□□□    □□□□□□□□
□□□□
□□□□
```

Check

My answers are reasonable, because $4 \times 4 = 16$ and $2 \times 8 = 16$.

Facts Divide.

7)49 = 7	5)25 = 5	3)27 = 9	3)24 = 8	9)9 = 1	3)12 = 4	4)16 = 4	2)10 = 5	6)42 = 7	4)28 = 7
6)0 = 0	2)4 = 2	5)35 = 7	2)6 = 3	3)15 = 5	6)54 = 9	2)16 = 8	8)72 = 9	5)30 = 6	3)21 = 7
3)9 = 3	9)81 = 9	5)40 = 8	4)20 = 5	7)56 = 8	2)18 = 9	6)36 = 6	8)56 = 7	2)12 = 6	7)42 = 6
6)48 = 8	2)14 = 7	4)36 = 9	4)24 = 6	5)45 = 9	2)8 = 4	3)18 = 6	7)63 = 9	4)32 = 8	8)64 = 8

Problem Solving Answer the question below.

Problem: Shae used a loop of string to form the triangle shown at right. If Shae uses the same loop of string to form a square, what will be the length of each side of the square? 3 in.

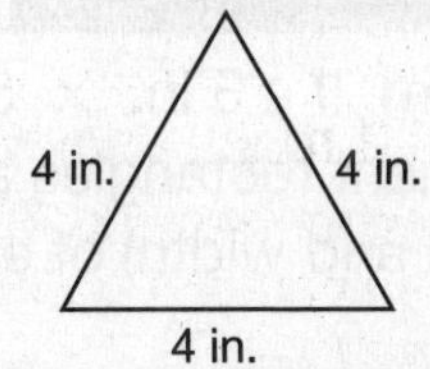

Understand

A loop of string is formed into a triangle that is 4 in. on each side.
I am asked to find the length of each side if the string is formed into a square.

Plan

I will first find the total length of the string. Then I will find how long each side would be if there were 4 sides.

Solve

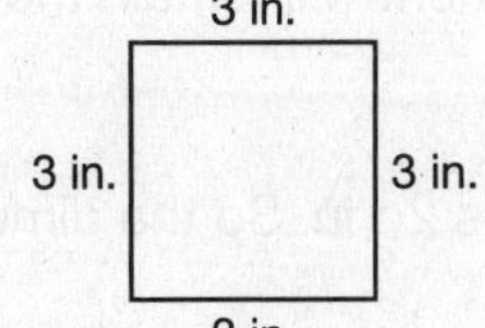

Total length of string: 4 in. + 4 in. + 4 in. = 12 in.
A square has 4 sides.
The side length of the square would be **3 in.**

Check

My answer is reasonable because 3 in. + 3 in. + 3 in. + 3 in. = 12 in.

Answers

Power-Up Test 12

Facts Divide.

$\overset{9}{9\overline{)81}}$	$\overset{6}{8\overline{)48}}$	$\overset{3}{6\overline{)18}}$	$\overset{5}{8\overline{)40}}$	$\overset{2}{3\overline{)6}}$	$\overset{4}{7\overline{)28}}$	$\overset{3}{5\overline{)15}}$	$\overset{8}{9\overline{)72}}$	$\overset{2}{7\overline{)14}}$	$\overset{5}{5\overline{)25}}$
$\overset{6}{9\overline{)54}}$	$\overset{4}{8\overline{)32}}$	$\overset{3}{4\overline{)12}}$	$\overset{0}{4\overline{)0}}$	$\overset{2}{6\overline{)12}}$	$\overset{4}{4\overline{)16}}$	$\overset{6}{7\overline{)42}}$	$\overset{2}{2\overline{)4}}$	$\overset{5}{9\overline{)45}}$	$\overset{7}{8\overline{)56}}$
$\overset{3}{8\overline{)24}}$	$\overset{7}{9\overline{)63}}$	$\overset{2}{4\overline{)8}}$	$\overset{4}{5\overline{)20}}$	$\overset{3}{3\overline{)9}}$	$\overset{5}{7\overline{)35}}$	$\overset{4}{9\overline{)36}}$	$\overset{2}{8\overline{)16}}$	$\overset{7}{7\overline{)49}}$	$\overset{1}{8\overline{)8}}$
$\overset{7}{6\overline{)42}}$	$\overset{2}{9\overline{)18}}$	$\overset{5}{6\overline{)30}}$	$\overset{3}{7\overline{)21}}$	$\overset{4}{6\overline{)24}}$	$\overset{2}{5\overline{)10}}$	$\overset{6}{6\overline{)36}}$	$\overset{8}{8\overline{)64}}$	$\overset{3}{9\overline{)27}}$	$\overset{8}{7\overline{)56}}$

Problem Solving Answer the question below.

Problem: If a 3 in. × 5 in. index card is folded as shown, two congruent rectangles are formed. What are the dimensions (length and width) of each rectangle? 3 in. × $2\frac{1}{2}$ in.

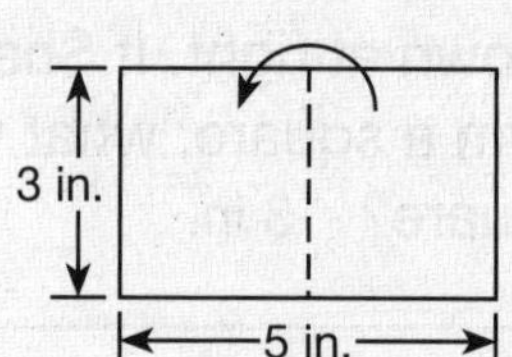

Understand

I know that a 3 in. × 5 in. index card is folded as shown in diagram.
I am asked to find the dimensions of the congruent rectangles that are formed.

Plan

I can use the diagram to visualize the problem. I need to find half of the 5 in. length. The 3 in. measurement will remain the same.

Solve

Half of 5 in. is $2\frac{1}{2}$ in. So the dimensions of each congruent half will be **3 in. × $2\frac{1}{2}$ in.**

Check

My answer is reasonable because only the 5 inch measurement is folded. The 3 inch measurement does not change.

Facts Divide.

$9\overline{)81}$ 9	$8\overline{)48}$ 6	$6\overline{)18}$ 3	$8\overline{)40}$ 5	$3\overline{)6}$ 2	$7\overline{)28}$ 4	$5\overline{)15}$ 3	$9\overline{)72}$ 8	$7\overline{)14}$ 2	$5\overline{)25}$ 5
$9\overline{)54}$ 6	$8\overline{)32}$ 4	$4\overline{)12}$ 3	$4\overline{)0}$ 0	$6\overline{)12}$ 2	$4\overline{)16}$ 4	$7\overline{)42}$ 6	$2\overline{)4}$ 2	$9\overline{)45}$ 5	$8\overline{)56}$ 7
$8\overline{)24}$ 3	$9\overline{)63}$ 7	$4\overline{)8}$ 2	$5\overline{)20}$ 4	$3\overline{)9}$ 3	$7\overline{)35}$ 5	$9\overline{)36}$ 4	$8\overline{)16}$ 2	$7\overline{)49}$ 7	$8\overline{)8}$ 1
$6\overline{)42}$ 7	$9\overline{)18}$ 2	$6\overline{)30}$ 5	$7\overline{)21}$ 3	$6\overline{)24}$ 4	$5\overline{)10}$ 2	$6\overline{)36}$ 6	$8\overline{)64}$ 8	$9\overline{)27}$ 3	$7\overline{)56}$ 8

Problem Solving Answer the question below.

Problem: Frank, Grey, Hala, and Inez will ride in the same car on the field trip. Three of the children will sit in the back seat of the car. What are the 4 possible combinations of three children? Use the abbreviations F, G, H, and I in your list. (*Hint*: The order of the children does not matter.) F-G-H, F-G-I, F-H-I; G-H-I

Understand

Frank, Grey, Hala, and Inez will ride in a car.
3 children will sit in the back seat.
I am asked to find the 4 possible combinations of three children. I will use the abbreviations F, G, H, and I.

Plan

I will make an organized list naming the combinations of children that will sit in the back seat. 3 children will sit in the back seat, so 1 child will not sit in the back seat. I can name the combination that excludes F, then the combination that excludes G, then the combination that excludes H, and then the combination that excludes I.

Solve

G-H-I (does not include F)
F-H-I (does not include G)
F-G-I (does not include H)
F-G-H (does not include I)

The 4 combinations are **F-G-H, F-G-I, F-H-I,** and **G-H-I.**

Check

My answers are reasonable because each combination contains 3 of the 4 children.

Answers

Power-Up Test 14

Facts Multiply.

$7 \times 9 = 63$	$4 \times 4 = 16$	$2 \times 5 = 10$	$6 \times 9 = 54$	$5 \times 6 = 30$	$3 \times 8 = 24$	$4 \times 9 = 36$	$2 \times 3 = 6$	$7 \times 8 = 56$	$3 \times 5 = 15$
$5 \times 9 = 45$	$3 \times 4 = 12$	$8 \times 9 = 72$	$2 \times 2 = 4$	$10 \times 10 = 100$	$4 \times 6 = 24$	$6 \times 7 = 42$	$2 \times 8 = 16$	$7 \times 7 = 49$	$8 \times 0 = 0$
$8 \times 8 = 64$	$2 \times 7 = 14$	$3 \times 6 = 18$	$5 \times 8 = 40$	$4 \times 7 = 28$	$3 \times 3 = 9$	$9 \times 9 = 81$	$5 \times 7 = 35$	$2 \times 9 = 18$	$7 \times 1 = 7$
$4 \times 5 = 20$	$6 \times 8 = 48$	$2 \times 4 = 8$	$0 \times 0 = 0$	$3 \times 7 = 21$	$4 \times 8 = 32$	$2 \times 6 = 12$	$5 \times 5 = 25$	$3 \times 9 = 27$	$6 \times 6 = 36$

Problem Solving Answer the question below.

Problem: Martin takes about 500 steps when he walks to the park from his house. In 5 steps, Martin travels about 12 feet. About how many feet does Martin travel when he walks to the park from his house? 1200 ft

Understand

500 steps from the house to the park
5 steps are 12 feet
I am asked to find about how many feet is 500 steps.

Plan

I can use an equal-groups pattern. I will find how many sets of 5 steps are in 500 steps. Then I will use that information to find the distance from the house to the park.

Solve

500 steps = 100 × 5 steps

500 steps = 100 × 12 feet = **1200 feet**

Check

My answer is reasonable because there are 100 sets of 5 steps in 500 steps. Each set of 5 steps is 12 feet, so 500 steps is 100 × 12 feet, or 1200 feet.

Facts Multiply.

$7 \times 9 = 63$	$4 \times 4 = 16$	$2 \times 5 = 10$	$6 \times 9 = 54$	$5 \times 6 = 30$	$3 \times 8 = 24$	$4 \times 9 = 36$	$2 \times 3 = 6$	$7 \times 8 = 56$	$3 \times 5 = 15$
$5 \times 9 = 45$	$3 \times 4 = 12$	$8 \times 9 = 72$	$2 \times 2 = 4$	$10 \times 10 = 100$	$4 \times 6 = 24$	$6 \times 7 = 42$	$2 \times 8 = 16$	$7 \times 7 = 49$	$8 \times 0 = 0$
$8 \times 8 = 64$	$2 \times 7 = 14$	$3 \times 6 = 18$	$5 \times 8 = 40$	$4 \times 7 = 28$	$3 \times 3 = 9$	$9 \times 9 = 81$	$5 \times 7 = 35$	$2 \times 9 = 18$	$7 \times 1 = 7$
$4 \times 5 = 20$	$6 \times 8 = 48$	$2 \times 4 = 8$	$0 \times 0 = 0$	$3 \times 7 = 21$	$4 \times 8 = 32$	$2 \times 6 = 12$	$5 \times 5 = 25$	$3 \times 9 = 27$	$6 \times 6 = 36$

Problem Solving Answer the question below.

Problem: Find the missing digits in this multiplication problem.

$$\begin{array}{r} 3\_ \\ \times \ \_ \\ \hline 3\_1 \end{array}$$

Understand

I am shown a multiplication problem with some missing digits. I am asked to find the missing digits.

Plan

I will work backwards and use logical reasoning and guess and check to find the missing digits.

Solve

I think:

"The multiplication is a number in the 30s times a single-digit number. The product is in the 300s."

"The bottom factor must be close to 10 for the product to be in the 300s. I can guess 9 for the bottom factor."

"What number times 9 equals a number that ends in 1?" (9)

"What is 39×9?" (351)

$$\begin{array}{r} 39 \\ \times \ 9 \\ \hline 351 \end{array}$$

Check

My answer is reasonable because $39 \times 9 = 351$.

Answers

Power-Up Test 16

Facts

Multiply.

7 × 9 63	4 × 4 16	2 × 5 10	6 × 9 54	5 × 6 30	3 × 8 24	4 × 9 36	2 × 3 6	7 × 8 56	3 × 5 15
5 × 9 45	3 × 4 12	8 × 9 72	2 × 2 4	10 × 10 100	4 × 6 24	6 × 7 42	2 × 8 16	7 × 7 49	8 × 0 0
8 × 8 64	2 × 7 14	3 × 6 18	5 × 8 40	4 × 7 28	3 × 3 9	9 × 9 81	5 × 7 35	2 × 9 18	7 × 1 7
4 × 5 20	6 × 8 48	2 × 4 8	0 × 0 0	3 × 7 21	4 × 8 32	2 × 6 12	5 × 5 25	3 × 9 27	6 × 6 36

Problem Solving

Answer the question below.

Problem: Henry is covering a 4-by-3 foot bulletin board with black and white construction paper squares, making a checkerboard pattern. Each square is 1 foot by 1 foot. Copy this diagram on your paper, and complete the checkerboard pattern. What is the total area of the bulletin board? How many squares of each color does Henry need? 12 sq. ft; 6 black and 6 white

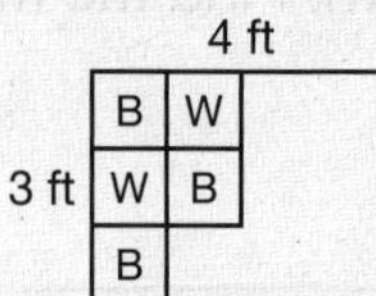

Understand

4-foot by 3-foot bulletin board
Checkerboard pattern
Each square is 1 foot by 1 foot.
I am asked to copy and complete the diagram.
I am asked to find the total area.
I am asked to find how many squares of each color are needed.

Plan

I will draw a diagram to show the checkerboard pattern. I can count the squares to find the area. I can also count the number of each color that is needed

Solve

The total area is **12 sq. ft.** Henry will need **6 black squares** and **6 white squares**.

4 ft (top); 3 ft (side)

B	W	B	W
W	B	W	B
B	W	B	W

Check

My answer is reasonable because 3 ft × 4 ft = 12 sq. ft. It makes sense that half of the 12 squares are white and half are black in the checkerboard pattern.

Facts Write these improper fractions as whole or mixed numbers.

$\frac{8}{3} = 2\frac{2}{3}$	$\frac{9}{3} = 3$	$\frac{3}{2} = 1\frac{1}{2}$	$\frac{4}{3} = 1\frac{1}{3}$	$\frac{7}{4} = 1\frac{3}{4}$
$\frac{10}{5} = 2$	$\frac{10}{9} = 1\frac{1}{9}$	$\frac{7}{3} = 2\frac{1}{3}$	$\frac{5}{2} = 2\frac{1}{2}$	$\frac{11}{8} = 1\frac{3}{8}$
$\frac{12}{12} = 1$	$\frac{9}{4} = 2\frac{1}{4}$	$\frac{12}{5} = 2\frac{2}{5}$	$\frac{10}{3} = 3\frac{1}{3}$	$\frac{16}{4} = 4$
$\frac{13}{5} = 2\frac{3}{5}$	$\frac{15}{8} = 1\frac{7}{8}$	$\frac{21}{10} = 2\frac{1}{10}$	$\frac{9}{2} = 4\frac{1}{2}$	$\frac{25}{6} = 4\frac{1}{6}$

Problem Solving Answer the question below.

Problem: Luis built this rectangular prism with small blocks.
How many small blocks did he use? 24 blocks

Understand

I am shown a picture of stacked blocks.
I am asked to find the total number of blocks in the shape.

Plan

I will use the diagram to count the blocks in layers.

Solve

In the top layer, I see 2 rows of 4 blocks each. This is a total of $2 \times 4 = 8$ blocks in the layer. There are 3 layers of blocks.

Total number of blocks: 3×8 blocks $=$ **24 blocks**

Check

My answer is reasonable because there are 3 layers of 8 blocks, which is a total of $8 + 8 + 8 = 24$ blocks.

Answers

Power-Up Test 18

Facts

Divide.

$\overset{3}{2\overline{)7}}$ R 1	$\overset{5}{3\overline{)16}}$ R 1	$\overset{3}{4\overline{)15}}$ R 3	$\overset{5}{5\overline{)28}}$ R 3	$\overset{5}{4\overline{)21}}$ R 1
$\overset{2}{6\overline{)15}}$ R 3	$\overset{2}{8\overline{)20}}$ R 4	$\overset{7}{2\overline{)15}}$ R 1	$\overset{8}{5\overline{)43}}$ R 3	$\overset{6}{3\overline{)20}}$ R 2
$\overset{4}{6\overline{)27}}$ R 3	$\overset{8}{3\overline{)25}}$ R 1	$\overset{8}{2\overline{)17}}$ R 1	$\overset{3}{3\overline{)10}}$ R 1	$\overset{4}{7\overline{)30}}$ R 2
$\overset{3}{8\overline{)25}}$ R 1	$\overset{2}{3\overline{)8}}$ R 2	$\overset{7}{4\overline{)30}}$ R 2	$\overset{6}{5\overline{)32}}$ R 2	$\overset{7}{7\overline{)50}}$ R 1

Problem Solving

Answer the question below.

Problem: List all the possible arrangements of the letters N, O and T. Bonus: What fraction of the arrangements spell words? NOT, NTO, ONT, OTN, TNO, TON;
Bonus: $\frac{1}{3}$

Understand

I am asked to list all the possible arrangements of the letters N, O, and T. I am also asked what fraction of the arrangements spell words.

Plan

I will make an organized list. I will list all the permutations that begin with N, then the permutations that begin with O, and then the permutations that begin with T.

Solve

Begin with N	Begin with O	Begin with O
NOT	ONT	TNO
NTO	OTN	TON

The possible arrangements are **NOT, NTO, ONT, OTN, TNO,** and **TON**.

Bonus: 2 of 6 arrangements are words (NOT and TON), so $\frac{1}{3}$ **of the arrangements spell words.**

Check

My answer is reasonable because each is an arrangement of the letters N, O, and T. I organized my list to find all the arrangements

Facts Write these improper fractions as whole or mixed numbers.

$\frac{8}{3} = 2\frac{2}{3}$	$\frac{9}{3} = 3$	$\frac{3}{2} = 1\frac{1}{2}$	$\frac{4}{3} = 1\frac{1}{3}$	$\frac{7}{4} = 1\frac{3}{4}$
$\frac{10}{5} = 2$	$\frac{10}{9} = 1\frac{1}{9}$	$\frac{7}{3} = 2\frac{1}{3}$	$\frac{5}{2} = 2\frac{1}{2}$	$\frac{11}{8} = 1\frac{3}{8}$
$\frac{12}{12} = 1$	$\frac{9}{4} = 2\frac{1}{4}$	$\frac{12}{5} = 2\frac{2}{5}$	$\frac{10}{3} = 3\frac{1}{3}$	$\frac{16}{4} = 4$
$\frac{13}{5} = 2\frac{3}{5}$	$\frac{15}{8} = 1\frac{7}{8}$	$\frac{21}{10} = 2\frac{1}{10}$	$\frac{9}{2} = 4\frac{1}{2}$	$\frac{25}{6} = 4\frac{1}{6}$

Problem Solving Answer the question below.

Problem: Two cups equal a pint. Two pints equal a quart. Two quarts equal a half gallon. Two half gallons equal a gallon. Halle poured 1 cup out of a pitcher that contained a half gallon of lemonade. How many cups of lemonade remained in the pitcher? 7 cups

Understand

Halle poured 1 cup out of a pitcher that contained a half gallon of lemonade.
I am asked to find how many cups remained in the pitcher.

Plan

I need to find the number of cups in a half gallon. Then I can subtract 1 cup.

Solve

1 half gallon = 2 quarts
= 2 × 2 pints = 4 pints
= 4 × 2 cups = 8 cups

1 half gallon is 8 cups, so pouring out 1 cup from the pitcher leaves 7 cups.

Check

My answer is reasonable because there are 2 × 2 = 4 cups in a quart, so there are 2 × 4 cups = 8 cups in a half gallon. Halle poured out 1 cup, which leaves 7 cups.

Answers

Power-Up Test 20

Facts

Reduce each fraction to lowest terms.

$\frac{2}{10} = \frac{1}{5}$	$\frac{3}{9} = \frac{1}{3}$	$\frac{2}{4} = \frac{1}{2}$	$\frac{6}{8} = \frac{3}{4}$	$\frac{4}{12} = \frac{1}{3}$
$\frac{6}{9} = \frac{2}{3}$	$\frac{4}{8} = \frac{1}{2}$	$\frac{2}{6} = \frac{1}{3}$	$\frac{3}{6} = \frac{1}{2}$	$\frac{6}{10} = \frac{3}{5}$
$\frac{5}{10} = \frac{1}{2}$	$\frac{3}{12} = \frac{1}{4}$	$\frac{2}{8} = \frac{1}{4}$	$\frac{4}{6} = \frac{2}{3}$	$\frac{50}{100} = \frac{1}{2}$
$\frac{2}{12} = \frac{1}{6}$	$\frac{8}{16} = \frac{1}{2}$	$\frac{9}{12} = \frac{3}{4}$	$\frac{25}{100} = \frac{1}{4}$	$\frac{6}{12} = \frac{1}{2}$

Problem Solving

Answer the question below.

Problem: The multiples of 7 are 7, 14, 21, 28, and so on. We can use multiples of 7 to count days of the week. For example, 29 days after Tuesday is Wednesday, since 29 days is 4 weeks plus 1 more day. Use the multiples of 7 to find the day of the week that is 68 days after Saturday. Thursday

Understand

Multiples of 7: 7, 14, 21, 28, ...
We can use multiples of 7 to count the days of the week.
I am asked to find the day of the week that is 68 days after Saturday.

Plan

I will find a multiple of 7 that is close to 68 and then count forward or backward from there.

Solve

68 is close to 70.
70 days after Saturday is Saturday.
69 days after Saturday is Friday.
68 days after Saturday is **Thursday.**

Check

I know that 63 days after Saturday is Saturday. I can count forward 5 days to find that 68 days after saturday is Thursday.

Facts

Write these improper fractions as whole or mixed numbers.

$\frac{8}{3} = 2\frac{2}{3}$	$\frac{9}{3} = 3$	$\frac{3}{2} = 1\frac{1}{2}$	$\frac{4}{3} = 1\frac{1}{3}$	$\frac{7}{4} = 1\frac{3}{4}$
$\frac{10}{5} = 2$	$\frac{10}{9} = 1\frac{1}{9}$	$\frac{7}{3} = 2\frac{1}{3}$	$\frac{5}{2} = 2\frac{1}{2}$	$\frac{11}{8} = 1\frac{3}{8}$
$\frac{12}{12} = 1$	$\frac{9}{4} = 2\frac{1}{4}$	$\frac{12}{5} = 2\frac{2}{5}$	$\frac{10}{3} = 3\frac{1}{3}$	$\frac{16}{4} = 4$
$\frac{13}{5} = 2\frac{3}{5}$	$\frac{15}{8} = 1\frac{7}{8}$	$\frac{21}{10} = 2\frac{1}{10}$	$\frac{9}{2} = 4\frac{1}{2}$	$\frac{25}{6} = 4\frac{1}{6}$

Problem Solving

Answer the question below.

Problem: Reggie scored 5 points in the first game and 9 points in the second game. How many points does Reggie need in the third game to achieve an average of 8 points per game? 10 points

Understand

1st game: 5 points
2nd game: 9 points
3 game average 8 points per game
I am asked to find the points needed in the 3rd game to achieve an average of 8 points per game.

Plan

I need to find the total score needed for an average of 8 points per game. Then I can write an equation to find how many more points are needed.

Solve

5 points + 9 points = 14 points

8-point-per-game average for 3 games is 3 × 8 points = 24 points altogether.

24 points − 14 points = 10 points

We find that Reggie needs to score **10 points** to raise his average to 8 points per game.

Check

My answer is reasonable because 5 + 9 + 10 = 24 and 24 ÷ 3 = 8.

Power-Up Test 22

Facts Simplify.

$\frac{6}{4} = 1\frac{1}{2}$	$\frac{10}{8} = 1\frac{1}{4}$	$\frac{9}{12} = \frac{3}{4}$	$\frac{12}{9} = 1\frac{1}{3}$	$\frac{12}{10} = 1\frac{1}{5}$
$\frac{12}{8} = 1\frac{1}{2}$	$\frac{8}{6} = 1\frac{1}{3}$	$\frac{10}{4} = 2\frac{1}{2}$	$\frac{8}{20} = \frac{2}{5}$	$\frac{20}{8} = 2\frac{1}{2}$
$\frac{24}{6} = 4$	$\frac{9}{6} = 1\frac{1}{2}$	$\frac{15}{10} = 1\frac{1}{2}$	$\frac{8}{12} = \frac{2}{3}$	$\frac{10}{6} = 1\frac{2}{3}$
$\frac{16}{10} = 1\frac{3}{5}$	$\frac{9}{12} = \frac{3}{4}$	$\frac{15}{6} = 2\frac{1}{2}$	$\frac{10}{20} = \frac{1}{2}$	$\frac{18}{12} = 1\frac{1}{2}$

Problem Solving Answer the question below.

Problem: Sandi will spin this spinner three times and write the result after each spin. List all the possible outcomes that Sandi could get with three spins. Make a tree diagram to help you find the outcomes. RRR, RRB, RBR, RBB, BRR, BRB, BBR, BBB

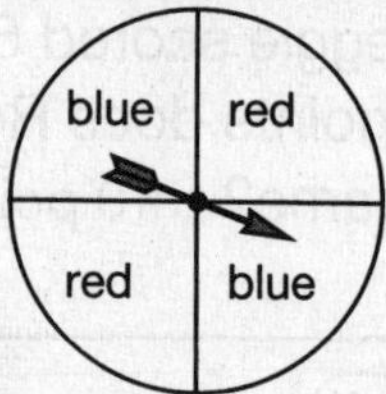

Understand

Two of the spinner sections are labeled "blue" and 2 are labeled "red."
I am asked to make a tree diagram to list the possible outcomes of three spins.

Plan

I will make a tree diagram. For each spin, the possible outcomes are R and B.

Solve

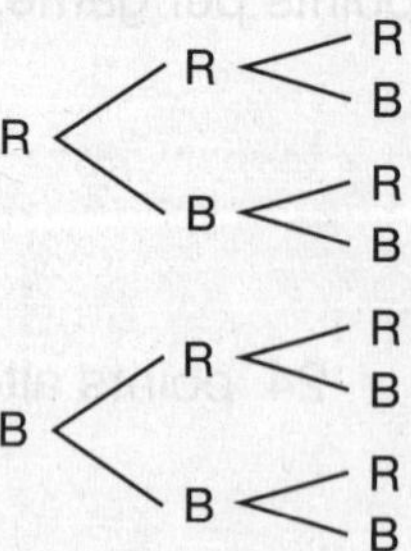

The possible outcomes are **RRR, RRB, RBR, RBB, BRR, BRB, BBR,** and **BBB.**

Check

My answers are reasonable because there are two outcomes for each spin: R or B. There are $2 \times 2 \times 2 = 8$ possible outcomes for 3 spins.

Facts Reduce each fraction to lowest terms.

$\frac{2}{10} = \frac{1}{5}$	$\frac{3}{9} = \frac{1}{3}$	$\frac{2}{4} = \frac{1}{2}$	$\frac{6}{8} = \frac{3}{4}$	$\frac{4}{12} = \frac{1}{3}$
$\frac{6}{9} = \frac{2}{3}$	$\frac{4}{8} = \frac{1}{2}$	$\frac{2}{6} = \frac{1}{3}$	$\frac{3}{6} = \frac{1}{2}$	$\frac{6}{10} = \frac{3}{5}$
$\frac{5}{10} = \frac{1}{2}$	$\frac{3}{12} = \frac{1}{4}$	$\frac{2}{8} = \frac{1}{4}$	$\frac{4}{6} = \frac{2}{3}$	$\frac{50}{100} = \frac{1}{2}$
$\frac{2}{12} = \frac{1}{6}$	$\frac{8}{16} = \frac{1}{2}$	$\frac{9}{12} = \frac{3}{4}$	$\frac{25}{100} = \frac{1}{4}$	$\frac{6}{12} = \frac{1}{2}$

Problem Solving Answer the question below.

Problem: How many 1-inch cubes would be needed to build a rectangular solid 4 inches long, 3 inches wide, and 2 inches high?

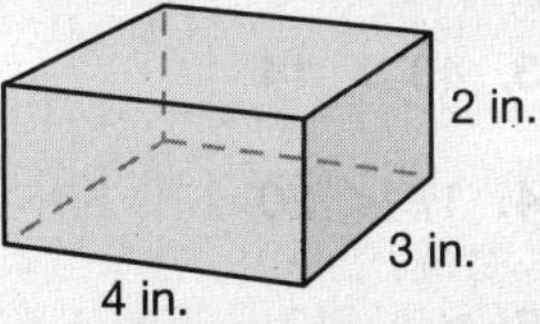

Understand

Length: 4 in.
Width: 3 in.
Height: 2 in.
I am asked to find how many 1-inch cubes would be needed to build the solid.

Plan

I can write an equation.

Solve

I can multiply the number of cubes along the edges.

$$4 \times 3 \times 2 = 24$$

24 1-inch cubes are needed.

Check

My answer makes sense because there would be 2 layers of 12 cubes each.

Cumulative Test 1A

1. 35, 42, 49
2. 56, 64, 72
3. 20, 16, 12
4. 6
5. even
6. **A.** 6789
7. **B.** 4576
8. **A.** 44
9. 823
10. 1
11. 290
12. 100
13. 40 > 14
14. 17 < 20
15. >
16. >
17. three hundred nineteen dollars and forty-five cents
18. four hundred nine
19. $613.80
20. 796

Cumulative Test 1B

1. 30, 36, 42
2. 45, 36, 27
3. 30, 33, 36
4. 4
5. odd
6. **A.** 3542
7. **C.** 2341
8. **B.** 30
9. 537
10. 6
11. 450
12. 10 tens
13. 15 < 50
14. 12 > 10
15. <
16. >
17. two hundred fifty-three dollars and fifteen cents
18. one hundred two
19. $440.14
20. 205

Cumulative Test 2A

1. 35 horses and buffalo
2. 20 minutes
3. $3 + 4 = 7$ $7 - 4 = 3$
$4 + 3 = 7$ $7 - 3 = 4$
4. 211,506
5. 543
6. 8
7. 27
8. 9
9. =
10. even
11. 4 people
12. 600
13. 508

14. 372

15. 23

16. $127

17. $267

18. 24

19. 40

20. 40

Cumulative Test 2B

1. 31 boys and girls

2. 15 girls

3. 4 + 6 = 10   10 − 6 = 4
   6 + 4 = 10   10 − 4 = 6

4. 408,911

5. 312

6. 9

7. 24

8. 4

9. =

10. even

11. 6 people

12. 770

13. 606

14. 454

15. 28

16. $83

17. $213

18. 28

19. 60

20. 36

Cumulative Test 3A

1. 9 + 8 = 17   17 − 9 = 8
   8 + 9 = 17   17 − 8 = 9

2. 28

3. −6 −5 −4 −3 −2 −1 0 1 2 3 4 5 6

4. A. ________

5. 7

6. 35 minnows and guppies

7. 15 strawberries

8. 卌 卌 |||

9. C. 5 × 1 = 5

10. 4 × 8

11. 268

12. $15.63

13. 1609

14. $1.72

15. 465

16. 0

17. 611,204

18. 27

19. >

20. 42

Cumulative Test 3B

1. 7 + 8 = 15   15 − 8 = 7
   8 + 7 = 15   15 − 7 = 8

2. 18

3. −5 −4 −3 −2 −1 0 1 2 3 4 5

4. C. ________

5. 6

6. 29 boys and girls

7. 9 points
8. ~~||||~~ ~~||||~~ |
9. **B.** $4 \times 1 = 4$
10. 5×6
11. 147
12. $8.18
13. 1656
14. $0.68
15. 355
16. 7
17. 21,350
18. 28
19. <
20. 56

Cumulative Test 4A

1. 351 coins
2. 42 dancers
3. 817
4. 244 men
5. ~~||||~~ ||||
6. <
7. <
8. **C.** ↕
9. even
10. $147
11. $8.76
12. 675
13. $28.08
14. 72
15. 5
16. 9
17. 6
18. 4
19. 82
20. 226

Cumulative Test 4B

1. 594 pages
2. 32 players
3. 609
4. 239 boys
5. ~~||||~~ ||
6. <
7. >
8. **A.** ⟷
9. odd
10. $215
11. $12.24
12. 1719
13. $15.27
14. 60
15. 4
16. 3
17. 6
18. 6
19. 81
20. 194

Cumulative Test 5A

1. 1, 2, 4, 8, and 16
2. 7 cans
3. 10 students
4. 5 students
5. $3 \times 7 = 21$ $\quad 21 \div 7 = 3$
   $7 \times 3 = 21$ $\quad 21 \div 3 = 7$
6. 1222
7. 24 mugs
8. <
9. **C.** $\frac{7}{15}$
10. $11.25
11. $2.72
12. 4
13. 7 R 2
14. 6
15. $46.17
16. 560
17. 2724
18. 5063
19. 1679
20. **C.** $3 \times (4 \times 5) = (3 \times 4) \times 5$

Cumulative Test 5B

1. 1, 2, 3, 6, 9, and 18
2. 7 students
3. 5 students
4. 2 students
5. $4 \times 5 = 20$ $\quad 20 \div 5 = 4$
   $5 \times 4 = 20$ $\quad 20 \div 4 = 5$
6. 1579
7. 28 desks
8. >
9. **B.** $\frac{12}{25}$
10. $17.50
11. $2.37
12. 4
13. 6 R 6
14. 9
15. $21.56
16. 480
17. 1472
18. 5896
19. 924
20. **A.** $2 + (3 + 4) = (2 + 3) + 4$

Cumulative Test 6A

1. 600 years
2. $6.00
3. 102
4. 8 ounces
5. 534
6. even
7. 5 people
8. −4°F
9. 1, 2, 3, 4, 6, 8, 12, and 24
10. 1608
11. $31.79
12. 175

13. 96 R 2

14. 50

15. $0.51

16. 1740

17. 84

18. $19.68

19. >

20. 9:20 p.m.

Cumulative Test 6B

1. 40 years

2. $3.60

3. 144

4. 3 pencils

5. 867

6. even

7. 3 people

8. –6°F

9. 1, 2, 4, 8, 16, and 32

10. 1806

11. $23.58

12. 185

13. 66 R 1

14. 75

15. $1.21

16. 1350

17. 90

18. $24.92

19. >

20. 7:50 a.m.

Cumulative Test 7A

1. 

2. 3:40 a.m.

3. 31 years

4. 1, 3, 5, and 15

5. 48 quarts

6. 60

7. 800

8. <

9. $\frac{1}{4}$

10. 25%

11. C.

12. 50

13. $18.46

14. $6.20

15. 2730

16. $55.00

17. 704

18. 72 R 3

19. 250

20. A.

Cumulative Test 7B

1.

2. 9:20 p.m.

3. 67 years

4. 1, 3, 7, and 21

5. 64 quarts

6. 80

7. 600

8. >

9. $\frac{3}{4}$

10. 75%

11. A.

12. 75

13. $19.36

14. $3.55

15. 1920

16. $50.00

17. 608

18. 73 R 3

19. 500

20. C.

Cumulative Test 8A

1. 39 orchids

2. $5\frac{2}{3}$

3. B.

4. (varies)

5. < (varies)

6. 800

7. 78°F

8. 132 pages

9. $\frac{7}{10}$

10. $807.71

11. 2637

12. 124,200

13. 560

14. $1.09

15. 91

16. 80 R 2

17. $43.45

18. 150

19. A. and C.

20. March 16, 2045

Cumulative Test 8B

1. 18 runners

2. $6\frac{2}{5}$

3. A.

4.

5. sample: =

6. 600

7. 54°F

8. 191 pages

9. $\frac{3}{7}$

10. $530.97

11. 2072

12. 103,500

13. 360

14. $1.07

15. 53

16. 90 R 3

17. $64.60

18. 91

19. B.  and C.

20. May 14, 2024

Cumulative Test 9A

1. **B.** It divides by 2.
2. 4
3. $2\frac{3}{8}$ inches
4. $22\frac{1}{2}$
5. **B.**
6. $1\frac{2}{3}$
7. 6 centimeters
8. 15%
9. >
10. 1014
11. $216.00
12. 175
13. $7.91
14. 902
15. 750
16. 4
17. $\frac{3}{10}$
18. 0
19. $0.73
20. 280 nickels

Cumulative Test 9B

1. **C.** It divides by 4.
2. 2
3. $1\frac{5}{8}$ inches
4. $12\frac{1}{2}$
5. **A.**
6. $1\frac{1}{3}$
7. 5 centimeters
8. 80%
9. <
10. 652
11. $242.80
12. 105
13. $12.62
14. 809
15. 150
16. 5
17. $\frac{7}{10}$
18. 0
19. $0.57
20. 400 dimes

Cumulative Test 10A

1. 10 pets
2. 87,009
3. 29 inches
4. 17 students
5. (varies); 75%
6. $2\frac{1}{2}$ inches
7. 300 centimeters
8. 304,011

9. $36.00

10. $8.18

11. 2064

12. $276.50

13. 117

14. 130 R 4

15. 860 R 4

16. 106

17. 0

18. $10\frac{4}{5}$

19. $2\frac{1}{4}$

20. Mary

Cumulative Test 10B

1. 41 years old

2. 5370

3. 70 inches

4. 16 students

5.  (varies); 75%

6. $2\frac{1}{4}$ inches

7. 20 millimeters

8. 125,364

9. $42.80

10. $36.25

11. 882

12. $304.80

13. 574

14. 140 R 3

15. 444 R 4

16. 108

17. 0

18. $5\frac{2}{3}$

19. $4\frac{2}{5}$

20. 2 more

Cumulative Test 11A

1. 8 horses

2. 3

3. 286 years

4. 330

5. 6 cm

6. 1

7. 18 inches

8. 16 people

9. 480,065

10. B. 

11. 4030

12. 347

13. $82.50

14. 2340

15. 902

16. 34

17. $3\frac{1}{3}$

18. $2\frac{2}{3}$

19. (varies); 75%

20. thirty-two million, one hundred eighty thousand, seven hundred ninety-five

Cumulative Test 11B

1. 7 players
2. 8
3. 109 years
4. 680
5. 8 cm
6. 0
7. 12 inches
8. 24 people
9. 308,403
10. **A.** 
11. 7934
12. 783
13. $50.00
14. 1610
15. 409
16. 32
17. $2\frac{3}{4}$
18. $2\frac{1}{2}$
19. 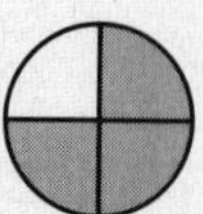 (varies); 75%
20. twenty-seven million, eight hundred forty-nine thousand, five hundred thirty-one

Cumulative Test 12A

1. $\frac{2}{5}$
2. 25
3. 96,011,241
4. 7
5. 8 bundles
6. 30 cm
7. 16 cm
8. $\frac{2}{5}$
9. **C.** likely
10. 4 questions
11. 3534
12. 903
13. 75,600
14. 255,670
15. 72 R 5
16. $1183\frac{3}{7}$
17. $0.31
18. 10
19. $\frac{6}{7}$
20. $6.42

Cumulative Test 12B

1. $\frac{2}{5}$
2. 95
3. 23,532,612
4. 9
5. 11 books
6. 24 cm
7. 10 cm
8. $\frac{3}{5}$
9. **B.** unlikely
10. 2 questions
11. 5139
12. 1575

13. 133,900

14. 69,920

15. 36 R 5

16. $1007\frac{1}{6}$

17. $0.16

18. 9

19. $\frac{3}{5}$

20. $5.02

Cumulative Test 13A

1. 40 chairs

2. $\frac{4}{5}$

3. 9 decades

4. 1200

5. 3300

6. **B.** $\angle AMC$

7. $5\frac{7}{10}$

8. $\frac{1}{6}$

9. **a.** 4 cm **b.** 14 cm

10. 8

11. 1

12. $1\frac{1}{3}$

13. $1\frac{2}{3}$

14. 5489

15. $0.22

16. 132,825

17. 1506 R 5

18. 21

19. hundredths

20. $6\frac{3}{4}$

Cumulative Test 13B

1. 16 students

2. $\frac{2}{3}$

3. 5 decades

4. 2800

5. 1700

6. **C.** $\angle BMC$

7. $3\frac{3}{10}$

8. $\frac{1}{6}$

9. **a.** 2 cm **b.** 6 cm

10. 9

11. 1

12. $2\frac{2}{3}$

13. $2\frac{3}{4}$

14. 3854

15. $2.25

16. 42,900

17. 870 R 4

18. 16

19. tenths

20. $4\frac{3}{5}$

Cumulative Test 14A

1. $2.69

2. 1, 2, 4, 8

3. **a.** $\frac{55}{100}$ **b.** 0.55

4. two hundred ninety and thirty-seven hundredths

5. 0.19

6. 8.7

7. 8

8. 4.6 cm

9. >

10. 3200

11. 4654

12. 624

13. 323,400

14. 602

15. 4200

16. 140

17. $1.64

18. $3\frac{4}{5}$

19. 10

20. $6\frac{1}{3}$

Cumulative Test 14B

1. $3.22

2. 1, 2, 4

3. a. $\frac{31}{100}$ b. 0.31

4. seventy-eight and forty-six hundredths

5. 0.23

6. 12.1

7. 7

8. 3.3 cm

9. >

10. 1800

11. 3148

12. 5742

13. 34,000

14. 809

15. 3000

16. 160

17. $2.18

18. $3\frac{2}{3}$

19. 7

20. $3\frac{1}{5}$

Cumulative Test 15A

1. $\frac{1}{3}, \frac{2}{4}, \frac{5}{8}, \frac{7}{7}$

2. $2\frac{3}{4}$

3. 10,560 feet

4. 8.04

5. 4

6. 5.01

7. a. $\frac{71}{100}$ b. 0.71 c. 71%

8. 3700

9. =

10. $22\frac{11}{40}$

11. $4.19

12. $1.49

13. 0.608

14. $6.51

15. $5\frac{9}{11}$

16. 8

17. 6 cm

18. 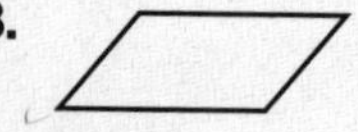 (varies)

19. 20 yd

20. 24 sq. yd

Cumulative Test 15B

1. $\frac{1}{3}, \frac{3}{6}, \frac{3}{4}, \frac{5}{5}$
2. $1\frac{4}{5}$
3. 108 inches
4. 12.21
5. 5
6. 10.61
7. **a.** $\frac{89}{100}$ **b.** 0.89 **c.** 89%
8. 2600
9. =
10. $31\frac{1}{30}$
11. $8.25
12. $0.46
13. 3.967
14. $2.70
15. $2\frac{2}{3}$
16. 5
17. 5 cm
18. (varies)
19. 18 yd
20. 20 sq. yd

Cumulative Test 16A

1. $12.20
2. 32
3. 0.83
4. 62,500 millimeters
5. 5000 grams
6. 8
7. =
8. $\frac{16}{24}$
9. 23 and 29
10. 3.3 cm
11. $35.52
12. 27.01
13. 22.75
14. 223
15. $19.28
16. 70,000
17. $4.41
18. $1\frac{1}{6}$
19. $\frac{7}{30}$
20. 18 mm

Cumulative Test 16B

1. $6.45
2. 27
3. 0.03
4. 850,000 centimeters
5. 48 ounces
6. 6
7. =
8. $\frac{9}{12}$
9. 7, 11, and 13
10. 2.3 cm
11. $22.26
12. 31.74
13. 26.85

14. 216
15. $17.25
16. 60,000
17. $5.75
18. $1\frac{2}{5}$
19. $\frac{3}{10}$
20. 20 mm

Cumulative Test 17A

1. **C.** 3
2. $\angle ADC$ (or $\angle CDA$)
3. $\overline{AB}$ (or $\overline{BA}$)
4. **A.** cone
5. **a.** 14 **b.** 7
6. 5 students
7. **a.** 8 **b.** $\frac{3}{4}$
8. 8 quarts
9. **a.** $\frac{2}{3}$ **b.** $\frac{3}{5}$ **c.** $\frac{1}{2}$
10. 149.459
11. 10.695
12. 64
13. $3.16
14. 164
15. 162,740
16. 34
17. $10\frac{2}{5}$
18. $1\frac{1}{4}$
19. =
20. 4 sq. cm

Cumulative Test 17B

1. **B.** 3
2. $\angle BCD$ (or $\angle DCB$)
3. $\overline{BC}$ (or $\overline{CB}$)
4. **B.** cylinder
5. **a.** 5 **b.** 15
6. 6 students
7. **a.** 7 **b.** $\frac{2}{3}$
8. 3000 milliliters
9. **a.** $\frac{3}{4}$ **b.** $\frac{1}{2}$ **c.** $\frac{2}{3}$
10. 210.153
11. 8.937
12. 125
13. $3.25
14. 26
15. 394,240
16. 94
17. $7\frac{1}{3}$
18. $2\frac{1}{3}$
19. =
20. 1 sq. cm

Cumulative Test 18A

1. 7:50 a.m.
2. $1\frac{3}{5}$
3. $\frac{3}{4}$
4. 500 milliliters
5. **B.** sphere
6. $\overline{DC}$ (or $\overline{CD}$)

7. $\angle ABC$ (or $\angle CBA$)

8. 14

9. 80

10. $\frac{6}{8}$

11. three hundred seventy-five thousandths

12. 15,962

13. 122,060

14. $5.89

15. $\frac{3}{8}$

16. 6

17. 1

18. $\frac{1}{3}$

19. $4\frac{2}{3}$

20. 32 mm

Cumulative Test 18B

1. 7:50 a.m.

2. $2\frac{1}{3}$

3. $\frac{2}{3}$

4. 2 quarts

5. **D.** rectangular solid

6. $\overline{AD}$ (or $\overline{DA}$)

7. $\angle BCD$ (or $\angle DCB$)

8. 9

9. 85

10. $\frac{4}{6}$

11. one hundred twenty-five thousandths

12. 32,859

13. 121,440

14. $1.58

15. $\frac{3}{16}$

16. 4

17. 1

18. $\frac{2}{3}$

19. $4\frac{3}{4}$

20. 60 mm

Cumulative Test 19A

1. $\frac{5}{4}$

2. $\frac{2}{14}, \frac{7}{14}, \frac{9}{14}$

3. 8 cars

4. **a.** 16 **b.** 32

5. **a.** $\frac{4}{5}$ **b.** 0.8 **c.** 80%

6. 0.2, $\frac{2}{3}$, 1

7. **a.** 3.3 centimeters **b.** 33 millimeters

8. $1\frac{1}{2}$

9. 12

10. 46.23

11. 848

12. $356.67

13. $1.30

14. 8

15. 51

16. $2\frac{1}{4}$

17. $6\frac{1}{3}$

18. $4\frac{1}{6}$

19. $12.44

20. $4.00

Cumulative Test 19B

1. $\frac{2}{3}$
2. $\frac{4}{12}, \frac{3}{12}, \frac{7}{12}$
3. 9 trees
4. **a.** 20 **b.** 40
5. **a.** $\frac{1}{2}$ **b.** 0.5 **c.** 50%
6. 0, 0.1, $\frac{1}{2}$
7. **a.** 2.2 centimeters **b.** 22 millimeters
8. $1\frac{2}{3}$
9. 6
10. 68.42
11. 157
12. $171.00
13. $1.20
14. 7
15. 42
16. $4\frac{2}{3}$
17. $5\frac{1}{2}$
18. $2\frac{2}{3}$
19. $23.40
20. $9.00

Cumulative Test 20A

1. *A*
2. $22.75
3. $\frac{3}{5}$
4. 250 millimeters
5. 6.5 cm
6. **a.** 1 pint $= \frac{1}{2}$ quart

   b. 1 quart $= \frac{1}{4}$ gallon

   c. 1 pint $= \frac{1}{8}$ gallon
7. 200,000
8. 400.203
9. $\frac{7}{9}$
10. $4\frac{1}{3}$
11. 7.03
12. 32
13. 13.099
14. $3.20
15. 9
16. 12 R 6
17. $\frac{1}{3}$
18. $\frac{10}{21}$
19. $1\frac{3}{5}$
20. 4

Cumulative Test 20B

1. *C*
2. $4.70
3. $\frac{2}{3}$
4. 800 centimeters
5. 6.4 cm
6. **a.** 1 cup $= \frac{1}{2}$ pint

   b. 1 pint $= \frac{1}{2}$ quart

   c. 1 cup $= \frac{1}{4}$ quart
7. 150,000
8. 5.07
9. $\frac{5}{7}$
10. $3\frac{2}{3}$
11. 9.65

12. 16

13. 4.146

14. $3.60

15. 10

16. 21 R 17

17. $2\frac{1}{3}$

18. $\frac{8}{9}$

19. $1\frac{1}{4}$

20. $1\frac{1}{2}$

Cumulative Test 21A

1. $49

2. **a.** 10 **b.** 8

3. 0.1, $\frac{2}{3}$, 2

4. 12 cars

5. 1.1 cm

6. rectangular solid

7. **A.**

8. 9.19

9. 8.34

10. 1.2

11. 4326

12. $4\frac{1}{3}$

13. $8\frac{1}{6}$

14. 1007

15. 31 R 23

16. $\frac{2}{5}$

17. 6

18. 12 cu. in.

19.

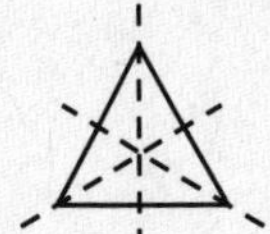

20. $\frac{1}{4}$

Cumulative Test 21B

1. $16

2. **a.** 13 **b.** 5

3. 0, 0.1, 1

4. 24 students

5. 1.2 cm

6. cylinder

7. **C.**

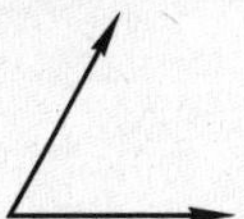

8. 9.65

9. 3.83

10. 1.8

11. 4380

12. $2\frac{1}{2}$

13. $5\frac{1}{2}$

14. 1002

15. 18 R 4

16. $\frac{2}{3}$

17. 2

18. 18 cu. in.

19. (varies)

20. $\frac{1}{5}$

Cumulative Test 22A

1. 2

2. 120 feet

3. **D.** 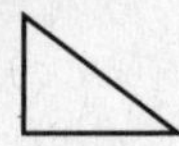

4. $\frac{1}{2}$

5. $\frac{2}{5}$

6. 16%

7. **a.** 3 **b.** 101

8. <

9. 44 cm

10. 121 sq. cm

11. 16.601

12. 2.4

13. 0.06

14. 1.02

15. 0.084

16. $4\frac{1}{7}$

17. $3\frac{3}{10}$

18. $6\frac{1}{3}$

19. $\frac{2}{7}$

20. 160 cu. in.

Cumulative Test 22B

1. 7

2. 300 feet

3. **B.** 

4. $\frac{2}{3}$

5. $\frac{1}{4}$

6. 30%

7. **a.** 7 **b.** 99

8. >

9. 48 in.

10. 144 sq. in.

11. 20.787

12. 1.5

13. 3.64

14. 0.36

15. 0.075

16. 7

17. 1

18. $7\frac{1}{2}$

19. $\frac{4}{9}$

20. 140 cu. in.

Cumulative Test 23A

1. 21

2. **D.** 0.05

3. −12°F

4. 16

5. *A*

6. (2,1)

7. $\frac{1}{2}$

8. **a.** 28 cm **b.** 22 sq. cm

9. $\frac{5}{2}$

10. 24

11. 21.00

12. 3.09

13. 40.5

14. 66 R 4

15. 234.5

16. 0.002

17. $3\frac{2}{3}$

18. $6\frac{3}{4}$

19. $\frac{3}{5}$

20. $\frac{2}{3}$

Cumulative Test 23B

1. 25
2. **B.** 0.05
3. –8°F
4. 10
5. *B*
6. (3, 3)
7. $\frac{1}{2}$
8. **a.** 18 cm **b.** 14 sq. cm
9. $\frac{8}{3}$
10. 30
11. 32.545
12. 6.64
13. 43.2
14. 27 R 5
15. 23.45
16. 0.001
17. $7\frac{1}{2}$
18. $4\frac{1}{2}$
19. $\frac{1}{3}$
20. $1\frac{1}{3}$

Benchmark Test 1

1. **B.** 3
2. **B.** 42 students
3. **C.** 3439
4. **C.** $7.65
5. **C.** Count up by sixes.
6. **D.** Friday
7. **A.** 7 people
8. **D.** 12 birds
9. **A.** 18
10. **C.** 1 fish
11. **D.** 376,103
12. **B.** Train 2
13. **C.** 4 miles
14. **B.** $3.75
15. **B.** –6
16. **D.** 162
17. **B.** 11 years old
18. **A.** 42 gallons
19. **D.** 15
20. **C.** 6×3
21. **B.** $3.85
22. **C.** 453
23. **B.** 154
24. **C.** $31.92
25. **D.** 2110

Benchmark Test 2

1. **B.** 50 years

2. **A.**

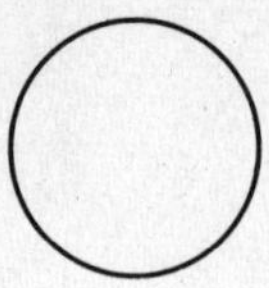

3. **C.** 108
4. **C.** 8
5. **A.** 900
6. **C.** 115 pages
7. **A.** 2
8. **B.** 450
9. **C.** 8
10. **B.** 2678
11. **C.** $12.62
12. **B.** 65 years
13. **A.** 1
14. **B.** 60
15. **B.** $1.50
16. **C.** 1400
17. **C.** 54
18. **B.** 420 ÷ 7
19. **C.** 7
20. **D.** 3 hr 45 min
21. **D.**

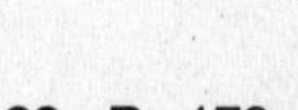

22. **B.** 179
23. **C.** $\frac{2}{2}$
24. **B.** 74
25. **A.** $31.28

Benchmark Test 3

1. **B.** $\frac{2}{5}$
2. **C.** 26
3. **B.** 20,607,025
4. **D.** 4
5. **B.** 10 books
6. **C.** 36 cm
7. **B.** 24 cm
8. **B.** 450
9. **B.** unlikely
10. **B.** 5
11. **C.** 842
12. **C.** 2646
13. **A.** 88,750
14. **B.** 129,600
15. **B.** 37 and 38
16. **B.** Point *B*
17. **B.** $0.32
18. **D.** $3\frac{4}{5}$
19. **A.** 81 in.
20. **D.** $6.76
21. **D.** obtuse
22. **D.** $2\frac{3}{4}$ in.
23. **C.** $1.44
24. **C.** 6 points
25. **A.** 25%

Benchmark Test 4

1. **B.** 7:55 a.m.
2. **C.** $3\frac{1}{3}$

3. **B.** $3.00

4. **C.** 0.7

5. **D.** $\overline{DA}$ and $\overline{CB}$

6. **B.** $\angle B$

7. **C.** 144 sq. ft

8. **C.** 7 inches

9. **A.** 12.37

10. **B.** 600 people

11. **B.** 1.012

12. **C.** 30,861

13. **D.** 110,160

14. **B.** $2.08

15. **A.** $\frac{3}{16}$

16. **A.** 2500 meters

17. **C.** 9 minutes

18. **D.** $\frac{2}{7}$

19. **A.** $\frac{3}{7}$

20. **D.** 6 cm

21. **B.** $3\frac{1}{3}$ cases

22. **B.** $24.50

23. **D.** 308

24. **A.** $2008\frac{3}{4}$

25. **A.** $4.79

Benchmark Test 5

1. **B.** $25

2. **A.** $\frac{2}{3}$ cake

3. **B.** $\frac{3}{5}$

4. **A.** $1\frac{1}{2}$ gallons

5. **D.** 0.208

6. **C.** $4 \times 4 \times 4$

7. **D.** rectangular solid

8. **B.** 27

9. **C.** 11

10. **A.** 3.5 kilometers

11. **C.** 7 minutes

12. **C.** 7

13. **D.** 25

14. **B.** $\frac{6}{12}$

15. **A.** 9

16. **D.** 1

17. **B.** 1

18. **C.** $\frac{3}{4}$

19. **B.** $5\frac{1}{2}$

20. **B.** reflection

21. **C.** $\frac{1}{3}$

22. **B.** 30 seeds

23. **A.** 8 minutes

24. **A.** 90

25. **C.** $2\frac{1}{2}$

Test Item No.	Saxon Math Intermediate 5 Benchmark Test Number				
	1	2	3	4	5
1.	B	B	B	B	B
2.	B	A	C	C	A
3.	C	C	B	B	B
4.	C	C	D	C	A
5.	C	A	B	D	D
6.	D	C	C	B	C
7.	A	A	B	C	D
8.	D	B	B	C	B
9.	A	C	B	A	C
10.	C	B	B	B	A
11.	D	C	C	B	C
12.	B	B	C	C	C
13.	C	A	A	D	D
14.	B	B	B	B	B
15.	B	B	B	A	A
16.	D	C	B	A	D
17.	B	C	B	C	B
18.	A	B	D	D	C
19.	D	C	A	A	B
20.	C	D	D	D	B
21.	B	D	D	B	C
22.	C	B	D	B	B
23.	B	C	C	D	A
24.	C	B	C	A	A
25.	D	A	A	A	C

End-of-Course Exam

1. **C.** 43
2. **B.** 9.67
3. **D.** 22.25
4. **A.** 45,600
5. **D.** 36¢
6. **B.** 6
7. **A.** $2\frac{1}{2}$
8. **C.** 6
9. **B.** $1\frac{1}{2}$
10. **C.** $\frac{2}{3}$
11. **D.** 6
12. **A.** 2,500,000
13. **C.** 20 millimeters
14. **B.** 1 meter
15. **D.** 0.2
16. **D.** 144
17. **C.** 10
18. **A.** 10.3
19. **B.** 280,000
20. **A.** 0.01, 0.1, 1.0
21. **C.** $\frac{3}{9}$
22. **D.** 45 miles
23. **B.** 23 students
24. **A.** 80
25. **B.** $\frac{1}{2}$
26. **C.** $6.36
27. **A.** 128 ounces
28. **B.** $13.75
29. **D.** $\frac{4}{5}$
30. **A.** 300 miles
31. **D.** 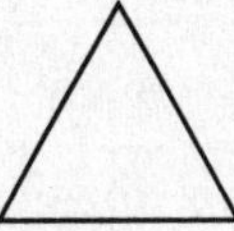
32. **C.** 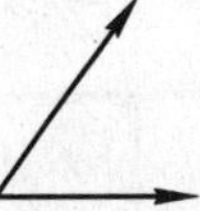
33. **B.** 70 mm
34. **B.** 20 inches
35. **C.** 96 sq. in.
36. **A.** $\frac{2}{5}$
37. **C.** 6
38. **D.** 
39. **A.** 
40. **C.** 9 sq. ft
41. **B.** $-2 < -1$
42. **A.** 27
43. **D.** 3
44. **D.** 5
45. **C.** $(6 \times 3) + (6 \times 4)$
46. **C.** 12
47. **A.** $\frac{1}{2} \times \frac{1}{2} < \frac{1}{2} + \frac{1}{2}$
48. **B.** 8
49. **C.** −3
50. **A.** Point *A*